WICKED PLANTS

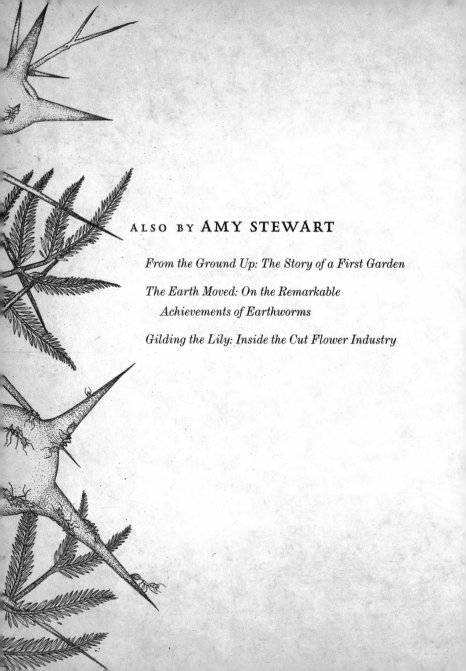

ALSO BY **AMY STEWART**

From the Ground Up: The Story of a First Garden

The Earth Moved: On the Remarkable
 Achievements of Earthworms

Gilding the Lily: Inside the Cut Flower Industry

Wicked Plants

THE A–Z OF PLANTS THAT KILL, MAIM, INTOXICATE AND OTHERWISE OFFEND

Amy Stewart

ETCHINGS BY **BRIONY MORROW-CRIBBS**
ILLUSTRATIONS BY **JONATHON ROSEN**

Timber Press
London

First published in 2009 by Algonquin Books of Chapel Hill.
This edition published in 2010 by Timber Press
2 The Quadrant
135 Salusbury Road
London NW6 6RJ
www.timberpress.co.uk

ISBN-13: 978-1-60469-127-6

Printed in the United States of America
Design by Anne Winslow, with thanks to Jean-Marc Troadee.

A catalogue record for this book is available from the British Library.

To PSB

Pinguicula spp.

"Look like the innocent flower,
But be the serpent under't."

—William Shakespeare, *Macbeth,* Act I, Scene 5

CONTENTS

CONTENTS

Consider Yourself Warned

A tree sheds poison daggers; a glistening red seed stops the heart; a shrub causes intolerable pain; a vine intoxicates; a leaf triggers a war. Within the plant kingdom lurk unfathomable evils.

In his 1844 story "Rappaccini's Daughter," Nathaniel Hawthorne described an elderly Italian doctor who tended a mysterious walled garden of poisonous plants. The old man's demeanor in the presence of his shrubs and vines "was that of one walking among malignant influences, such as savage beasts, or deadly snakes, or evil spirits, which, should he allow them one moment of license, would wreak upon him some terrible fatality." The story's hero, young Giovanni, watched from a window and found it most disturbing "to see this air of insecurity in a person cultivating a garden, that most simple and innocent of human toils."

Innocent? This is how Giovanni viewed the luxuriant vegetation below his window, and it is how most of us approach our gardens and the plants we encounter in the wild: with a kind of naïve trust. We would never pick up a discarded coffee cup from the pavement and drink from it, but on a walk we'll nibble unfamiliar berries as if they had been placed there for our appetites alone. We'll brew a medicinal tea from unrecognizable bark and leaves that a friend passes along, assuming that anything natural must be safe. And when a baby comes home, we rush to add safety caps to electrical outlets but ignore the houseplant in the kitchen and the shrub by the front door.

You can garden for years without ever suffering the ill effects of a plant like monkshood, whose cheerful blue flowers conceal a toxin that brings on death by asphyxiation. You can walk for miles and never encounter the coyotillo shrub, whose berries cause a slow but deadly paralysis. But someday the plant kingdom's dark side may make itself known to you. When it does, you should be prepared.

I DIDN'T WRITE this book to scare people away from the outdoors. Quite the opposite is true. I think that we all benefit from spending more time in nature—but we should also understand its power. I live on the rugged northern California coast, and every summer the Pacific Ocean sneaks up behind a family enjoying a day at the beach and claims a life. Those of us who live here know that so-called sleeper waves can kill with no warning. I love the ocean, but I never turn my back on it. Plants deserve the same kind of guarded respect. They can nourish and heal, but they can also destroy.

Some of the plants in this book have quite a scandalous history. The extract of castor bean plant killed a BBC journalist. A weed sent British soldiers crazy for eleven days. A toxic tree temporarily blinded Captain Cook's crew. Poison hemlock killed Socrates, and the most wicked weed of all—tobacco—has claimed ninety million lives. A stimulating little bush in Colombia and Bolivia called *Erythroxylum coca* has fueled a global drug war, and hellebore was used by the ancient Greeks in one of the earliest instances of chemical warfare.

Plants that are monstrously ill mannered deserve recognition, too: kudzu has devoured cars and buildings in the American South, and a seaweed known as killer algae escaped from Jacques Cousteau's aquarium in Monaco and continues to smother ocean floors around the world. The horrid corpse flower reeks of dead bodies; the carnivorous *Nepenthes truncata* can devour a mouse; and the whistling thorn acacia harbors an army of aggressive ants that attack anyone who comes near the tree. Even a few interlopers from outside the plant kingdom—hallucinogenic mushrooms, toxic algae—merit inclusion here for their wicked ways.

If this book entertains, alarms, and enlightens you, I've done my job. I'm not a botanist or a scientist but rather a writer and a gardener who is fascinated by the natural world. These are the most fascinating and evil plants from among thousands that grow around the world. If you're in the market for a comprehensive poisonous plant identification guide, I've included a special section for you in the bibliography. And if you suspect that someone has been poisoned by a plant, please do not spend precious time flipping through this book in search of symptoms or a diagnosis. While I describe the possible or probable effects of many toxins, their potency can vary widely depending on the plant's size, the time of day, the temperature, the part of the plant in question, and how it was ingested. Don't try to figure it out on your own. Instead, seek immediate medical attention.

Finally, do not experiment with unfamiliar plants or take a plant's power lightly. Wear gloves in the garden; think twice before sampling a berry from the hedgerow or throwing a root into the saucepan. If you have small children, teach them not to put plants in their mouths. If you have pets, remove the temptation of poisonous plants from their environment. The nursery industry is woefully lax about identifying poisonous plants; let your garden center know that you'd like to see sensible, accurate labeling of plants that could harm you. Use reliable sources to identify poisonous, medicinal, and edible plants. (A great deal of misinformation circulates on the Internet, with tragic consequences.) I did not shy away from including plants that intoxicate, but I included them to provide a warning, not an endorsement.

I CONFESS THAT I am enchanted by the plant kingdom's criminal element. I love a good villain, whether it is an enormous specimen of *Euphorbia tirucalli,* the pencil cactus with corrosive sap that raises welts on the skin, on display at a garden show, or the hallucinatory moonflower, *Datura inoxia,* blooming in the desert. There is something beguiling about sharing their dark little secrets. And these secrets don't just lurk in a remote jungle. They're in our own back gardens.

WICKED PLANTS

Aconite

ACONITUM NAPELLUS

In 1856 a dinner party in the Scottish village of Dingwall came to a horrible end. A servant had been sent outside to dig up horseradish, but instead he uprooted aconite, also called monkshood. The cook, failing to recognize that she had been handed the wrong ingredient, grated it into a sauce for the roast and promptly killed two priests who were guests at the dinner. Other guests were sickened but survived.

Even today, aconite is easily mistaken for an edible herb. This sturdy, low-growing herbaceous perennial is found in gardens and in the wild throughout Europe and the United States. The spikes of blue flowers give the plant its common name "monkshood" because the uppermost sepal is shaped like a helmet or a hood. All parts of the plant are extremely toxic. Gardeners should wear gloves anytime they go near it, and backpackers should not be tempted by its white, carrot-shaped root. The Canadian actor Andre Noble died of aconite poisoning after he encountered it on a hiking trip in 2004.

FAMILY: Ranunculaceae

HABITAT: Rich, moist garden soil, temperate climates

NATIVE TO: Europe

COMMON NAMES: Wolfsbane, monkshood, leopard's bane

The poison, an alkaloid called aconitine, paralyzes the nerves, lowers the blood pressure, and eventually stops the heart. (Alkaloids are organic compounds that in many cases have some kind of pharmacological effect on humans or animals.) Swallowing the plant or its roots can bring on severe vomiting and then death by asphyxiation. Even casual skin contact can cause numbness, tingling, and cardiac symptoms. Aconitine is so powerful that Nazi scientists found it useful as an ingredient for poisoned bullets.

Nazi scientists found aconite useful as an ingredient for poisoned bullets.

In Greek mythology, deadly aconite sprang from the spit of the three-headed hound Cerberus as Hercules dragged it out of Hades. Legend has it that it got another of its common names, wolfsbane, because ancient Greek hunters used it as a bait and arrow poison to hunt wolves. Its reputation as a witch's potion from the Middle Ages earned it a starring role in the Harry Potter series, where Professor Snape brews it to assist Remus Lupin in his transformation to a werewolf.

Meet the Relatives Related to aconite are the lovely blue and white *Aconitum cammarum;* the delphinium-like *A. carmichaelii;* and the yellow *A. lycoctonum,* commonly referred to as wolfsbane.

ARROW POISONS

Indigenous tribes in South America and Africa have used toxic plants as arrow poisons for centuries. The poisonous sap of a tropical vine, rubbed onto an arrowhead, makes a potent tool for both warriors and hunters. Many arrow poisons, including the tropical vine curare, cause paralysis. The lungs stop working, and eventually the heart stops beating, but there are often no outward signs of agony.

CURARE *Chondrodendron tomentosum*

A sturdy, woody vine found throughout South America. It contains a powerful alkaloid called d-tubocurarine that acts as a muscle relaxant. Useful for hunters, it rapidly immobilizes prey, even causing birds to fall from the trees. Any game caught using arrows poisoned with curare would be safe to eat, because the toxin is only effective when it enters the bloodstream directly, as opposed to the digestive tract.

If the animal (or enemy) is not slaughtered right away, death comes within a few hours as paralysis reaches the respiratory system.

Experiments on animals poisoned in this manner have shown that once breathing stops, the heart continues to beat for a short time, even though the poor creature appears dead.

The power of this drug was not lost on nineteenth- and twentieth-century physicians, who realized that it could be used to hold a patient still during surgery. Unfortunately, it did nothing to relieve the pain, but it would allow a doctor to go about his work without the distraction of a patient's thrashing about. As long as artificial respiration was maintained throughout the surgery to keep the lungs functioning, the curare would eventually wear off and leave no long-lasting side effects. In fact, an extract from the plant was used in combination with other anesthesia throughout most of the twentieth century, but new, improved drugs have taken its place.

The word *curare* has also been used to refer more generally to a wide variety of arrow poisons derived from plants, including:

STRYCHNINE VINE   *Strychnos toxifera*

A South American vine closely related to the strychnine tree, *Strychnos nux-vomica*. Like curare, it causes paralysis. In fact, the two were often used in combination.

KOMBE   *Strophanthus kombe*

A native African vine containing a cardiac glycoside that goes directly to work on the heart. While a powerful dose may stop the heart, extracts have also been used as a cardiac stimulant to treat heart failure or irregular heartbeats. Nineteenth-century plant explorer Sir John Kirk obtained specimens of the plant to bring back to the Royal Botanic Garden at Kew and inadvertently participated in a medical experiment: he accidentally got a little juice from the plant on his toothbrush and reported a quick drop in his pulse rate after he brushed his teeth.

UPAS TREE
Antiaris toxicaria

A member of the mulberry family native to China and other parts of Asia. The bark and leaves produce a highly toxic sap. Charles Darwin's grandfather Erasmus claimed that the tree's fumes could kill anyone who went within miles of it. Although this is only legend, references to the noxious fumes of the upas tree can be found in the writings of Charles Dickens, Lord Bryon, and Charlotte Brontë. A character in a Dorothy L. Sayers novel once described a serial killer as "first cousin to an upas tree." Like other arrow poisons, the sap contains a powerful alkaloid that can stop the heart.

> *Charles Darwin's grandfather Erasmus claimed that the upas tree's fumes could kill anyone who went within miles of it.*

POISON ARROW PLANT
Acokanthera spp.

An appropriately named shrub native to South Africa that also kills by attacking the heart. Some reports show that it was used in a particularly devious way: the juice was smeared on the sharp seeds of puncture vine (*Tribulus terrestris*). The seeds grow in the sturdy shape of a caltrop, which is a simple spiked weapon with two or more legs that always lands with one spike pointed up. Metal versions of these weapons have been used since Roman times; it was easy to fling them in the path of an approaching enemy. Puncture vine seeds smeared with the juice of *Acokanthera* would have been an efficient way to embed the poison in the feet of an attacker, and the half-inch-long spines would slow them down considerably.

Ayahuasca Vine

BANISTERIOPSIS CAAPI

and Chacruna

PSYCHOTRIA VIRIDIS

William Burroughs drank ayahuasca tea in the jungle and reported his findings to Allen Ginsberg. Alice Walker sought it out, as did Paul Theroux, Paul Simon, and Sting. It has been the subject of a patent dispute, a Supreme Court case, and a number of drug raids.

The bark of the woody ayahuasca vine, brewed with the leaves of the chacruna shrub, form a potent tea called ayahuasca (or, alternatively, hoasca). Chacruna contains the powerful psychoactive drug DMT (dimethyltryptamine), a Schedule I controlled substance, but the leaves must be activated by another plant, usually *Banisteriopsis caapi*, before the effects can be felt. The latter contains a naturally occurring monoamine oxidase inhibitor, similar to the compounds found in prescription antidepressants. Put the two together, and you're in for a mind-altering experience.

BANISTERIOPSIS CAAPI

FAMILY:
Malpighiaceae

HABITAT:
Tropical forests in South America

NATIVE TO:
Peru, Ecuador, Brazil

COMMON NAMES:
Yage, caapi, natem, dapa

One of the best-known religious groups to use the tea is União do Vegetal, or UDV. Its ceremonies usually last for several hours and are closely supervised by a more experienced member of the church. Participants experience bizarre hallucinations; one described it this way: "Dark creatures sail by. Tangles of long, hissing serpents. Dragons spitting fire. Screaming humanlike forms."

The experience usually ends with severe vomiting. The vomiting is seen as a kind of purge of psychological problems or demons. People who have participated in the ceremony report that it relieved their depression, cured their addiction, or treated other medical problems. Although there is little clinical evidence to support this, ayahuasca's similarity to prescription antidepressants has interested some researchers, who have called for more detailed studies.

The tea also attracted the attention of Jeffrey Bronfman, a member of the wealthy family that founded Seagram, makers of whisky and gin. Bronfman formed a branch of the UDV church in the United States and began importing the tea. In 1999 his shipment was intercepted by U.S. Customs agents, and Bronfman sued to have the tea returned to him. The case landed in the Supreme Court, and in 2006 the court ruled in his favor, allowing the use of the tea for religious purposes. The court's ruling was based primarily on the Religious Freedom Restoration Act, which Con-

PSYCHOTRIA VIRIDIS

FAMILY:
Rubiaceae

HABITAT:
Lower levels of the Amazon; also found in other parts of South America

NATIVE TO:
Brazil

COMMON NAMES:
Chacrona

> *"Dark creatures sail by.*
> *Tangles of long, hissing serpents,*
> *dragons spitting fire. Screaming*
> *humanlike forms."*

gress had passed in response to an earlier Supreme Court ruling against the use of peyote for religious purposes. According to news reports, the church, known as Centro Espírita Beneficente União do Vegetal, has 130 members and meets at Bronfman's home in Santa Fe. The U.S. Drug Enforcement Administration continues to enforce the laws against nonreligious use of ayahuasca and other products containing DMT.

Meet the Relatives *Banisteriopsis caapi* is a member of a large family of flowering shrubs and vines found primarily in South America and the West Indies.

Meet the Relatives *Psychotria viridis* is a member of the coffee family; relatives include cinchona, the quinine tree, and the poisonous ground cover sweet woodruff, which flavors may wine. Another powerful vine in the same genus is *P. ipecacuanha,* from which a treatment for plant poisonings, syrup of ipecac, is made.

Betel Nut

ARECA CATECHU

The betel nut palm rises gracefully to over thirty feet tall on a slim, dark green trunk, sports glossy dark leaves, and produces lovely white flowers that perfume tropical breezes. This palm is also responsible for the betel nut, an addictive stimulant that turns teeth black and saliva red. Four hundred million people around the world consume it.

The custom of chewing betel nuts dates back thousands of years. Seeds from 5000 to 7000 BC have been found in a cave in Thailand, and a skeleton from 2680 BC was found in the Philippines with teeth stained by the juice of the betel nut.

FAMILY:
Arecaceae

HABITAT:
Tropical forests

NATIVE TO:
Malaysia

COMMON NAMES:
Betel palm, areca, pinang

Like coca, the betel nut is stashed between the cheek and gum and is usually mixed with a little something extra to give it a kick. In India thin slices of the nut are wrapped in a fresh betel leaf with some slaked lime (calcium hydroxide extracted from ashes), a few Indian spices, and sometimes tobacco. The betel leaf used for the outer wrapping is the leaf of *Piper betle*, or "betel" vine, a low-growing perennial whose leaves are also a stimulant. In fact, the betel nut palm gets its name from its association with this unrelated, but synergistic, plant.

This packet of leaf and nut, often called a quid, has a bitter, peppery taste, and it releases alkaloids similar to nicotine. Users get an energy boost, a mild high, and more saliva than they know what to do with.

There's only one way to handle the constant flow of red saliva from your mouth when you chew betel: spit it out (swallowing causes nausea). In countries where betel nuts are popular, the sidewalks are stained with red saliva. If this sounds unpleasant, consider poet and essayist Stephen Fowler's description: "There is an almost orgasmic satisfaction to be found in the experience of saliva-ducts open to full throttle. Delicious above all is the aftermath: when the chew is finished, your mouth is left astonishingly fresh and sweet. You feel uniquely cleansed, drained, and purified."

> *There's only one way to handle the constant flow of red saliva from your mouth when you chew betel: spit it out.*

The betel nut is enjoyed throughout India, Vietnam, Papau New Guinea, China, and in Taiwan, where the government is trying to crack down on "betel nut beauties," scantily clad women who sit in roadside stands and sell their products to truck drivers.

In addition to its addictive qualities—withdrawal symptoms include headaches and sweats—regular chewing of betel nuts leads to an increased risk of mouth cancer and may also contribute to asthma and heart disease. The use of betel is largely un-regulated around the world, and public health officials worry that it could rival tobacco as a serious health threat.

Meet the Relatives   The betel nut palm is perhaps the best-known member of the Areca genus, which contains about fifty different species of palms. Its partner in crime, *Piper betle,* is related to *P. nigrum,* the source of black pepper, and *P. methysticum,* source of the mellow herbal supplement kava.

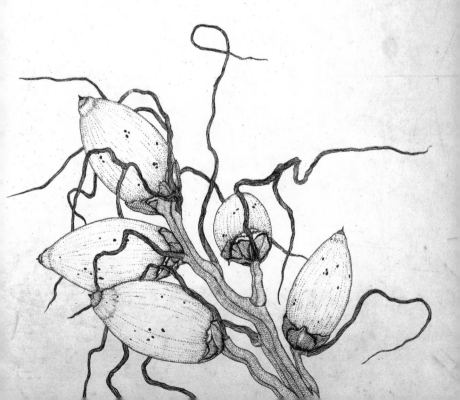

Castor Bean

RICINUS COMMUNIS

One autumn morning in 1978, communist defector and BBC journalist Georgi Markov walked across London's Waterloo Bridge and stood waiting at a bus stop. He felt a painful jab in the back of his thigh and turned around in time to see a man pick up an umbrella, mumble an apology, and run away. Over the next few days, he developed a fever, had trouble speaking, began throwing up blood, and finally went to the hospital, where he died.

The pathologist found hemorrhages in almost every organ in his body. He also found a small puncture mark on Markov's thigh and a tiny metal pellet in his leg. The pellet contained ricin, the poisonous extract of the castor bean plant. Although KGB agents were suspected of the crime, no one has ever been charged with the infamous "umbrella murder."

Castor bean is a dramatic annual or tender perennial shrub with deeply lobed leaves, prickly seedpods, and large, speckled seeds. Some of the more popular garden varieties sport red stems and splashes of burgundy on the leaves. The plant can reach over ten feet tall in a single growing season and will grow into a substantial bush if it is not killed by a winter freeze. Only

FAMILY:
Euphorbiaceae

HABITAT:
Warm, mild winter climates, rich soil, sunny areas

NATIVE TO:
Eastern Africa, parts of western Asia

COMMON NAMES:
Palma Christi, ricin

Although KGB agents were suspected of the crime, no one has ever been charged with the infamous "umbrella murder."

the seeds are poisonous. Three or four of them can kill a person, although people do survive castor seed poisoning, either because the seeds aren't well chewed or because they are purged quickly.

Castor oil has been a popular home remedy for centuries. (The ricin is removed during the manufacturing process.) A spoonful of the oil is an effective laxative. Castor oil packs are used externally to soothe sore muscles and inflammation. It's also used in cosmetics and other products.

But even this natural vegetable oil is not entirely benign: in the 1920s Mussolini's thugs used to round up dissidents and pour castor oil down their throats, inflicting a nasty case of diarrhea on them. Sherwood Anderson described the castor oil torture this way: "It was amusing to see Fascisti, wearing black shirts and looking very earnest, bottles sticking out of their hip pockets, chasing wildly down the street after a shrieking Communist. Then the capture, the terrible assault, hurling the luckless Red to the sidewalk, injecting the bottle into his mouth to the muffled accompaniment of blasphemy of all the gods and devils in the universe."

Meet the Relatives The garden spurge called euphorbia, known for its irritating sap; the poinsettia, also mildly irritating but, contrary to rumor, not dangerous; and the rubber tree, *Hevea brasiliensis,* source of natural rubber, are all related to the castor bean.

ORDEAL POISONS

Among nineteenth-century European explorers a story circulated about the existence of a West African bean that could determine a person's guilt or innocence. According to local custom, the accused would swallow the bean, and what happened next would determine the outcome of the trial. If he vomited the bean, he was innocent, and if he died, he was guilty and got what he deserved. A third alternative existed: he could purge the nut, or evacuate it through his bowels, in which case he was also determined guilty and sold into slavery as punishment. (A thriving slave trade dating back to the early 1500s facilitated this quirk in the West African criminal justice system.)

This practice was known as trial by ordeal, and plants used for the trials were called ordeal beans. Several plants were used; judges could choose a less toxic plant when they wanted to influence the outcome in favor of the accused.

CALABAR BEAN *Physostigma venenosum*

The ordeal poison of choice, the Calabar bean flourishes in warm, tropical climates; reaches up to fifty feet in height; and produces lovely red blossoms like those of the scarlet runner bean, followed by long, fat seedpods and hefty dark brown beans.

The alkaloid physostigmine is responsible for the bean's toxic effects. It works like nerve gas, disrupting the lines of communication between nerves and muscles. The result is copious saliva, seizures, and loss of control over bladder and bowels; eventually, as it becomes impossible to control the respiratory system, death by asphyxiation will occur.

Its chemical composition, along with a little armchair psychology, may explain why the plant had such different effects on the poor souls facing a trial by ordeal. A person who knew they were innocent might chew the bean quickly and swallow it with pride, ingesting a quick dose that would cause them to vomit before the bean could do more damage. A guilty party, dreading death, might take tiny, slow bites. Ironically, this attempt to prolong their own life would only hasten their death by delivering a gradual, well-digested dose of poison.

By the 1860s Calabar beans were the talk of London. Dr. James Livingstone returned from Africa with an account of a poison he called *muave* and noted that tribal chiefs would volunteer to drink the *muave* to prove their innocence, their strength of character, or to demonstrate that they had not been the victim of witchcraft. Mary Kingsley, a pioneering explorer who broke many taboos by traveling alone to previously unexplored parts of Africa, wrote in 1897 about an oath some tribal members would make before taking an ordeal poison they called Mbiam: "If I have been guilty of this crime . . . Then, Mbiam! THOU deal with me!"

These frightening chants did not stop intrepid British scientists from testing the beans on themselves. In an 1866 London *Times* story titled "Scientific Martyrdom," Sir Robert Christison is described as having come "very near killing himself in testing the effect of the recently introduced Calabar bean upon his own organism . . . and was as nearly face to face with death as a man well can be and yet escape its jaws."

TANGHIN POISON-NUT
Cerbera tanghin

Employed in Madagascar, this relative to the suicide tree *Cerbera odollam* is poisonous in all parts; even smoke from the burning wood can be toxic. However, the nuts deliver the poison in the most convenient form for trial by ordeal.

SASSY BARK OR CASCA BARK
Erythrophleum guineense or *E. judiciale*

Observed in use along the banks of the Congo, the curvy, reddish-brown bark of this tree is toxic enough to stop the heart. Ranchers know to keep their cattle away from it, because it could even kill a steer. Other names for the tree include "ordeal bark" and "doom bark."

STRYCHNINE TREE
Strychnos nux-vomica

The seed of the strychnine tree is a potent enough poison to make it useful as an ordeal bean. Any prisoner offered *nux vomica* seeds to prove their innocence would be well advised to do some fast talking and suggest another ordeal poison, because the strychnine is far more likely to cause convulsions and death by asphyxiation than vomiting.

UPAS TREE
Antiaris toxicaria

This Indonesian tree produces a toxic sap that's also useful as an arrow poison. It was once (falsely) believed to produce narcotic fumes, and tales circulated that prisoners were being put to death simply by tying them to the upas tree and letting its sap and fumes slowly poison the condemned.

Coca

ERYTHROXYLUM COCA

In 1895 Sigmund Freud wrote to a colleague that "a cocainization of the left nostril had helped me to an amazing extent." A modest, medium-sized shrub had transformed Freud's entire outlook on life. "In the last few days I have felt quite unbelievably well," he wrote, "as though everything had been erased . . . I have felt wonderful, as though there never had been anything wrong at all."

Archaeological evidence shows that coca leaves were placed between the cheek and gum as a mild stimulant as early as 3000 BC. When the Incas came into power in Peru, the ruling class seized control of the coca supply, and when Spanish conquistadores arrived in the sixteenth century, the Catholic Church banned the use of the devilish plant. Eventually, practical considerations won out, and the Spanish government realized that it would be better off regulating and taxing the use of coca, while making it available to slaves who had been forced to work in gold and silver mines. The Spaniards found that, with enough coca, the natives could work quickly, for long hours, with very little food. (Never mind the fact that most died after a few months of this treatment.)

FAMILY:
Erythroxylaceae

HABITAT:
Tropical rain forest

NATIVE TO:
South American

COMMON NAME:
Cocaine

21

An Italian doctor named Paolo Mantegazza promoted the medicinal and recreational use of the leaves of the coca plant in the mid-nineteenth century. He was so enthralled by his discovery that he wrote: "I sneered at the poor mortals condemned to live in this valley of tears while I, carried on the wings of two leaves of coca, went flying through the spaces of 77,438 words, each more splendid than the one before . . ."

Cocaine, an alkaloid that can be extracted from coca leaves, has been used as an anesthetic, a pain reliever, a digestive aid, and an all-around health tonic. Trace amounts were present in early versions of the soft drink Coca-Cola; while the company's recipe is a closely guarded secret, coca extract is still believed to be a flavoring, just without the cocaine alkaloid.

The coca plant's ability to inspire humans to go to war, both against each other and against the plant, may be its most deadly quality.

The leaves are legally imported by an American manufacturer, which buys it from Peru's National Coca Company, transforms it into Coca-Cola's secret flavoring, and extracts the cocaine for pharmaceutical use as a topical anesthetic.

The coca plant's ability to inspire humans to go to war, both against each other and against the plant, may be its most deadly quality. A healthy shrub can produce three crops a year of fresh, glossy leaves. The cocaine and other alkaloids in the leaves serve as a natural pesticide, helping to ensure that the plant flourishes even when it's under attack. Although a few different species can be used to extract cocaine, the plant used most often for this purpose is *Erythroxylum coca,* which grows along the eastern slope of the Andes mountain range.

In native Andean communities, coca leaves are still chewed as a mild stimulant. Some pharmacological studies suggest that this provides a much milder and nonaddicting stimulation that works on a different part of the brain than cocaine does. The leaves are surprisingly nutritious and very high in calcium, prompting a minister in Bolivia's new pro-coca government to suggest that instead of milk, coca leaves should be fed to schoolchildren.

The shrub has also survived attacks from another kind of enemy: the drug war's aerial spraying of the herbicide glyphosate. Drug eradication programs have been foiled by a new, resistant variety of coca called *Boliviana negra.* It emerged, apparently, without any help from scientists in laboratories. Instead, naturally resistant plants have simply been discovered in the fields and passed from farmer to farmer.

Advocates of traditional coca farming point out that coca is an Andean crop dating back several thousand years, while cocaine was invented in Europe 150 years ago. The problems created by cocaine use, they suggest, should be solved within those countries and not at the expense of the coca plant.

Meet the Relatives *Erythroxylum coca* is the best-known member of this family of angiosperms, but *E. novagranatense* also contains the cocaine alkaloid. *E. rufum,* or false cocaine, can be found in some botanical gardens in the United States.

Coyotillo

KARWINSKIA HUMBOLDTIANA

Coyotillo is a modest shrub of the Texas plains, rarely reaching more than five or six feet in height. The bright green, untoothed leaves and pale green flowers make it an entirely forgettable shrub. But the round black berries it produces in fall would be impossible to forget.

Coyotillo berries contain a compound that causes paralysis—but not immediately. The unlucky subject may not realize that he or she has been poisoned for several days or even weeks. But then, the paralysis sets in—and if this were a murder mystery, it would happen just as the unlucky victim was driving through a dark mountain pass or trying to sneak past the jewelry store's security alarm. What author could invent a more devious drug?

FAMILY:
Rhamnaceae

HABITAT:
Dry southwestern desert

NATIVE TO:
American West

COMMON NAMES:
Tullidora, cimmaron, palo negrito, capulincillo

Animals have been known to lose control over their hind legs, or to lurch backward for no reason they could understand, under the influence of this harmless-looking berry. In the laboratory, administering just the right dose to animals would cause quadriplegia. Livestock browsing freely on the shrub could eventually lose control of their limbs entirely, and death would not be far behind.

Coyotillo goes to work on the feet first and then moves to the lower legs. Once the limbs are still, it brings the respiratory system to a halt, and then it silences the tongue and throat. The plant thrives along the border between Texas and Mexico. Ironically, the name *coyotillo* is the diminutive of the Spanish word *coyote,* given to a person who helps illegal immigrants make the dangerous border crossing into the United States. One study counted about fifty people in Mexico who died from eating the berries during a two-year period.

> *Once the limbs are still, coyotillo brings the respiratory system to a halt, and then it silences the tongue and throat.*

Coyotillo thrives in the canyons and dry riverbeds of southern Texas, New Mexico, and northern Mexico, where it can tolerate the mean heat and scorched earth. Give it the right conditions and it may reach twenty feet, the size of a small tree.

Meet the Relatives   Coyotillo is a member of the buckthorn family; many shrubs in this family play host to butterflies. Most produce berries, but they don't pose the same threat.

THIS HOUSEPLANT COULD BE YOUR LAST

Some of the most popular houseplants are surprisingly toxic. They were chosen not for their suitability as a snack for pets and small children, but for their ability to thrive in a year-round climate of 50 to 70 degrees Fahrenheit. That's why many houseplants are actually tropical plants that come from the jungles of South America and Africa.

The poinsettia, one of the most reviled indoor plants, is not nearly as toxic as its reputation would lead one to believe. As a member of the Euphorbiaceae family, the sap is mildly irritating, but that is the extent of it. While the poinsettia gets plenty of bad press around the holidays, many other houseplants escape notice in spite of their more toxic qualities.

27

PEACE LILY   *Spathiphyllum* spp.

A South American plant with simple white flowers that resemble calla lilies. In 2005 more people called poison control centers about possible peace lily poisoning than any other plant. (This may have more to do with how popular the plant is than how poisonous it is.) The plant contains calcium oxalate crystals that can bring on skin irritation, burning of the mouth, difficulty swallowing, and nausea.

ENGLISH IVY   *Hedera helix*

This ubiquitous European vine grows outdoors as a ground cover but is also one of the most popular indoor potted plants. The berries are bitter enough to discourage people from eating them, but they could cause severe gastrointestinal problems and possible delirium or respiratory problems. Sap from the leaves can cause serious skin irritation and blisters.

PHILODENDRON   *Philodendron* spp.

An ivylike plant native to South America in the West Indies. All parts of the plant contain calcium oxalates. Nibbling on a leaf might only bring about mild burning in the mouth or a little nausea, but ingesting it could lead to severe abdominal pain, and repeated skin contact may cause serious allergic reactions. Poison control centers in the United States got over sixteen hundred calls in 2006 related to philodendron poisoning.

DIEFFENBACHIA OR DUMB CANE   *Dieffenbachia* spp.

A tropical South American plant well known for its ability to temporarily inflame vocal cords, leaving people unable to speak. Some species are believed to have been used as an arrow poison in combination with other plants. Most poisonings involve severe irritation of the mouth and throat, swelling of the tongue and face, and stomach problems. The sap is also irritating to the skin, and can cause light sensitivity and pain if it gets in the eyes.

FICUS TREE AND RUBBER TREE   *Ficus benjamina, F. elastica*

These two indoor trees are closely related species in the mulberry family. The latex from these plants can provoke severe allergic reactions. One case history describes a woman who developed anaphylactic shock and other frightening symptoms that disappeared promptly after her ficus tree was removed from her home.

PENCIL CACTUS OR MILKBUSH   *Euphorbia tirucalli*

This African plant is not actually a cactus, but it gets its name from the long, skinny stems that resemble a succulent. Pencil cactus has become popular in modern interior design for its striking, architectural shape. But like other euphorbia, it produces a corrosive sap that causes severe rashes and eye irritation. It requires some pruning to keep it down to a reasonable size indoors, and gardeners are often surprised that a single pruning session can bring on such a painful reaction.

JERUSALEM CHERRY OR
CHRISTMAS CHERRY   *Solanum pseudocapsicum*

Often sold as an ornamental pepper plant, it is actually more closely related to deadly nightshade. All parts of the plant contain an alkaloid that can bring on weakness, drowsiness, nausea and vomiting, and heart problems.

Deadly Nightshade

ATROPA BELLADONNA

Professor and plant researcher Henry G. Walters speculated in 1915 about the potential for cross-breeding carnivorous and poisonous plants. He believed that if a poisonous plant had "the semimuscular system possessed by the carnivorous plants, it would be more dangerous than the cholera." Dr. Walters declared that plants were capable of love and that they had memories, implying that they might also hold a grudge as lovers do. The deadly nightshade, he believed, was filled with hatred.

Although the entire plant is poisonous—just rubbing up against it can raise pustules on the skin—the black berries are the plant's most tempting feature. A Virginia farmer named Charles Wilson lost his children to those berries in 1880. The youngsters' terse obituary suggests an agonizing weekend: "The first and youngest died last Thursday, the second, on Sunday night, and the third, and only remaining child, on Monday."

Even today, tales of deadly nightshade poisoning appear in the medical literature. An elderly woman turned up at the hospital

FAMILY:
Solanaceae

HABITAT:
Shady, damp areas; seeds need uniformly damp soil to germinate

NATIVE TO:
Europe, Asia, north Africa

COMMON NAMES:
Belladonna, devil's cherry, dwale (an Anglo-Saxon word meaning "a stupefying or soporific drink")

every fall in a kind of psychosis; doctors were unable to trace the cause of her hallucinations, delusions, and headaches. After several days, the symptoms would subside on their own. Finally, her daughter brought in a handful of berries from a shrub growing near her house. She had been snacking on deadly nightshade every autumn when the berries grew ripe but somehow managed to escape a fatal poisoning.

"Hot as a hare, blind as a bat, dry as a bone, red as a beet, and mad as a hatter."

This is far from the only case: A couple earned their place in medical history by baking a pie of nightshade berries, mistaking them for the much more edible bilberries. In Turkey, a review of nightshade poisoning found that forty-nine children were sickened over a six-year period. Most ate the berries themselves out of curiosity, but at least one child was fed nightshade by his parents in the mistaken hope that it would treat his diarrhea.

Deadly nightshade performs its dark magic with the help of an alkaloid called atropine, which causes rapid heartbeat, confusion, hallucinations, and seizures. The symptoms are so unpleasant that atropine is sometimes added to potentially addictive painkillers to keep patients from getting hooked. Medical students memorize this simple mnemonic trick to help them recognize the signs of poisoning: "Hot as a hare, blind as a bat, dry as a bone, red as a beet, and mad as a hatter." "Madness" in this case refers to meaningless speech, a sign of deadly nightshade poisoning.

The herbaceous perennial is found across Europe, Asia, and North America, where it flourishes in damp, shady spots. It grows to about three feet tall, producing pointed, oval-shaped leaves and purplish brown tubular flowers. From these flowers the bright black berries emerge, beginning as hard green fruit that ripen to red, finally reaching their full dark glory in the fall.

Early physicians mixed up a potent brew of deadly nightshade, hemlock, mandrake, henbane, opium, and other herbs as a surgical anesthetic. Atropine still has medicinal uses today and has been administered as an antidote to poisoning from nerve gas and pesticide exposure.

Italian women dropped mild tinctures of deadly nightshade into their eyes to dilate their pupils, which they thought made them more alluring. The name "belladonna" may come from this practice; it means "beautiful woman," but the term might also originate from *buona donna,* a medieval witch doctor who treated the indigent with mysterious potions.

Atropa comes from one of the three Fates of Greek mythology. Each Fate had a role in determining human destiny. Lachesis measured the thread of destiny at birth; Clotho spun the thread, controlling one's destiny; and then, at the end, Atropos brought death at the time and manner of her choosing. Milton remembered her this way:

Comes the blind Fury with the abhorrèd shears,
And slits the thin-spun life.

Meet the Relatives   Member of the large and unruly Solanaceae family, which includes henbane, mandrake, datura, and the spicy Habanero chile pepper.

Death Camas

ZIGADENUS VENENOSUS, OTHERS

Several species of death camas thrive in meadows across the western United States. They are bulb plants with strappy, grasslike leaves and clusters of starry flowers in shades of pink, white, or yellow. The entire plant contains toxic alkaloids, and although the level of toxins may vary between species, it is safest to assume that they are all highly poisonous. Eating any part of the plant or the bulb will cause drooling or frothing at the mouth, vomiting, extreme weakness, an irregular pulse, and confusion and dizziness. In cases of severe poisoning, the final symptoms include seizures, coma, and death.

Death camas poisoning is a serious problem for livestock. Sheep tend to be drawn to the plant, especially in the early spring when there isn't anything else to eat. If the ground is wet, they are often able to pull up the entire plant. There is no treatment for animals who have been sickened, and usually they are simply found dead.

Dietitian and food historian Elaine Nelson McIntosh recently discovered that death camas might have played a role in the terrible illnesses that members of the Lewis and Clark expedition faced. In September 1805 the group passed through the Bitterroot

FAMILY: Melanthiaceae

HABITAT: Meadows

NATIVE TO: North America, primarily in the West

COMMON NAMES: Black snakeroot, star lily

Eventually Lewis and Clark's team staggered on, facing a winter in which they would be forced to eat their dogs and take their chances with the roots of other unfamiliar plants.

Mountains, a particularly difficult range of the Rockies. They were already desperately low on food and suffering from a variety of nutrition related ailments, including dehydration, sore eyes, rashes, boils, and wounds that would not heal. On September 22 the group managed to obtain some food from the Nez Perce tribe. It included dried fish and the roots of a similar plant, blue camas (*Camassia* spp.), both of which the men had eaten before with no problem.

Members of the group were beset with violent illness and suffered from diarrhea and vomiting. Lewis himself was seriously ill for two weeks. Dr. McIntosh believes that the men may have been inadvertently poisoned by eating death camas instead of the edible blue camas. The flowers would not have been in bloom at the time, making it difficult to distinguish the two, and even local Indians familiar with the bulbs could have made an honest mistake. The expedition came to a halt while the men recovered. Eventually they staggered on, facing a winter in which they would be forced to eat their dogs and take their chances with the roots of other unfamiliar plants.

Meet the Relatives   Once classified in the lily family, death camas is now grouped into a family with other wild bulbs, many of them poisonous. Relatives include false hellebore (*Veratrum album*) and trillium (*Trillium* spp.).

DEADLY DINNER

What do corn, potatoes, beans, and cashews have in common? They can all be poisonous under the right circumstances. Some of the world's most important food crops contain toxic compounds that require them to be cooked or combined with other foods to make them safe. Some, like the grass pea, have earned a world wide reputation for turning a famine into an even more tragic catastrophe.

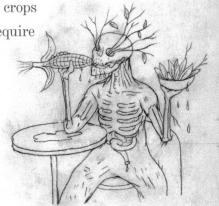

GRASS PEA *Lathyrus sativus*

Also called chickling vetch, this pea has been a dietary staple in the Mediterranean, Africa, India, and parts of Asia for centuries. Like most legumes, it is an excellent source of protein, but it has one serious drawback: it contains a neurotoxin called beta-N-oxalyl-diamino propionic acid, or beta-ODAP. The first symptom of beta-ODAP poisoning, or lathyrism, is a weakening of the legs. Eventually, the toxin kills nerve cells and victims become paralyzed from the waist down. Without treatment, they will die.

How has this pea remained such a popular ingredient in flours, porridges, and stews? If they are soaked for a long time in water or fermented in breads or pancakes, they pose little risk. Grass peas are one of the few food crops that can survive a serious drought. People are then left with little else to eat — and not enough water to soak the peas in.

Hippocrates warned that people who "ate peas continuously became impotent in the legs." Today one of the great tragedies of famines in places like Ethiopia and Afghanistan is that the high-protein pea is typically reserved for men to give them strength so that they can feed their families. Instead, it has the opposite effect, reducing them to crawling on their knees (and as one report noted, "Wheelchairs aren't an option for most lathyrism sufferers, as they tend to live in dirt-floor huts"). Even if the drought receded and they stopped eating the peas, they might still be disabled for life.

Francisco Goya depicted the ravages of lathyrism in his circa 1810 aquatint print called *Gracias a la Almorta,* or "Thanks to the Grass Pea." He was portraying a grueling outbreak that occurred during Spain's war for independence against Napoleon's army.

The grass pea resembles a sweet pea. It is a climbing vine with fine tendrils and blue, pink, purple, or white flowers. It is often used as a fodder crop for cattle, and still shows up in the cuisine of many countries around the world.

CORN *Zea mays*

Native people in the Americas knew how to prepare this local crop safely. Traditional recipes called for adding slaked lime or calcium hydroxide, a naturally occurring mineral, to corn. (The basic recipe for tortillas still includes the addition of lime.) Without it, the niacin in corn cannot be absorbed. This is not a problem unless corn is eaten by itself and makes up most of a person's diet. When that happens—as it did with early settlers who did not understand the risks—the result is a severe niacin deficiency called pellagra.

As early as 1735, when corn was imported from the New World, impoverished people in Spain and other European countries showed symptoms of pellagra. Those symptoms came to be known as the four D's: dermatitis, dementia, diarrhea, and death. In fact, a pair of researchers writing for a British medical journal suggested that the ghastly symptoms of pellagra could have inspired European myths of vampirism in Bram Stoker's *Dracula:* pale skin that erupted in blisters when exposed to the sun, sleepless nights brought on by dementia, an inability to eat normal food because of digestive problems, and a morbid appearance just before death.

During the first half of the twentieth century, pellagra sickened three million Americans and killed one hundred thousand. The disease was not entirely understood until the 1930s. Today corn is considered to be a perfectly safe and healthy part of the diet as long as it is eaten in combination with other foods.

RHUBARB *Rheum x hybridum*

The leaves of this Asian plant contain high levels of oxalic acid, which can cause weakness, difficulty breathing, gastrointestinal problems, and even coma and death in rare circumstances. In 1917 the *Times* of London reported on the death of a minister who died after eating a dish made from rhubarb leaves. The unfortunate cook admitted that she had used a recipe that she found in the newspaper titled "War Time Tip from the National Training Schools of Cookery." In fact, there was a war on, and food was scarce, but recipes like this one added yet another threat to both soldiers and civilians.

ELDERBERRY

Sambucus spp.

This fruit, popular in jams, cakes, and pies, is much more dangerous when consumed raw. In 1983 a group of people attending a retreat in central California had to be flown by helicopter to a hospital after drinking fresh elderberry juice. Most parts of the plant, including the uncooked fruit, may contain varying levels of cyanide. Generally, people experience severe nausea and recover.

CASHEW

Anacardium occidentale

There's a reason why grocery stores don't sell raw cashew nuts. Cashews are part of the same botanical family as poison ivy, poison oak, and poison sumac. The cashew tree produces the same irritating oil, urushiol. The nut itself is perfectly safe to consume, but if it comes into contact with any part of the shell during harvest, it will give the person who eats it a nasty rash. For that reason, cashews are steamed open, making them partially cooked even if they appear to be raw. In 1982 a Little League team in Pennsylvania sold bags of cashew nuts that were imported from Mozambique. Half of the people who ate them developed rashes on their arms, groin, armpits, or buttocks because some of the bags of nuts contained pieces of cashew shells, which would have had the same effect as mixing poison ivy leaves with the nuts.

RED KIDNEY BEAN

Phaseolus vulgaris

Perfectly safe and healthy, except if eaten raw or undercooked. The harmful compound in kidney beans is called phytohaemagglutinin, and it can bring on severe nausea, vomiting, and diarrhea. People usually recover quickly, but it takes only four or five raw beans to bring on these extreme symptoms. The incomplete cooking of raw beans in a slow cooker is a common source of red kidney bean poisoning.

POTATO
Solanum tuberosum

This member of the dreaded nightshade family contains a poison called solanine, which can bring on burning and gastrointestinal symptoms and even coma and death in rare cases. Cooking a potato will kill most of the solanine in it, but if a potato has been exposed to the light long enough for its skin to turn green, that may be a sign of increased levels of solanine.

ACKEE
Blighia sapida

The ackee fruit plays an essential role in Jamaican cuisine. Only the aril (the flesh surrounding the seeds) is safe to eat, and the fruit must be harvested at a precise point of ripeness or it may be toxic. Ackee poisoning, or Jamaican vomiting sickness, can be fatal if untreated.

CASSAVA
Manihot esculenta

An important food crop in Latin America, Asia, and parts of Africa, the root is cooked in much the same way that potatoes are. A starchy flour derived from the root is used to make tapioca pudding and bread. There's just one problem: cassava contains a substance called linamarin that converts to cyanide in the body. The cyanide can be eliminated through careful preparation that involves soaking, drying, or baking the root, but this process is imperfect and can take several days. In times of drought, cassava roots may produce higher levels of the toxin, and people in famine-stricken areas may eat more of the root and take less care with preparation.

Cassava poisoning can be deadly. Even at lower levels it can cause a chronic condition known in Africa as konzo. Symptoms include weakness, tremors, a lack of coordination, vision problems, and partial paralysis.

Ergot

CLAVICEPS PURPURA

Historians still wonder what caused the bizarre behavior that led eight young girls to be suspected of demonic possession and witchcraft during the winter of 1691 in Salem, Massachusetts. One girl after another went into convulsions, babbled incoherently, and complained of creepy skin sensations. Doctors could find nothing wrong with them, and the best explanation medical science had to offer was that a witch cast a spell over the girls.

Almost three hundred years later, a researcher had another idea. Ergot, the toxic fungus that infects rye and contaminates bread, could explain the girls' bizarre behavior.

Ergot is a parasitic fungus that attaches itself to a flowering cereal grass like rye or wheat. It flourishes in damp conditions and possesses the special trick of being able to mimic the very grain it has infected. It forms a hardened mass called a sclerotium on its host and can nurture dormant spores until the conditions are just right to release them. Millions of ergot spores can be harvested right along with a rye or wheat crop, and the

FAMILY:
Clavicipitaceae

HABITAT:
Thrives on cereal crops such as rye, wheat, and barley

NATIVE TO:
Europe

COMMON NAMES:
Ergot of rye, St. Anthony's fire

43

bread produced from those grains can contain enough of the fungus to infect whoever eats it—including some young girls living in Salem during a particularly damp winter.

The alkaloids in ergot constrict blood vessels, causing seizures, nausea, uterine contractions, and eventually gangrene and death. Long before Albert Hofmann extracted lysergic acid from ergot to

---

This "dancing mania" was also sometimes called St. Anthony's fire, a possible reference to the awful burning sensations ergot victims felt, and the eventual gangrenous blisters and peeling skin.

---

make LSD, people infected with ergotism had bad LSD-like trips of their own. Hysteria, hallucinations, and a feeling that something is crawling on the skin are all signs of ergot poisoning.

Records going back to the Middle Ages show that from time to time, an entire village would succumb to mysterious illness. Villagers would dance in the streets, go into convulsions, and eventually collapse. This "dancing mania" was also sometimes called St. Anthony's fire, a possible reference to the awful burning sensations victims felt, and the eventual gangrenous blisters and peeling skin. The disease is believed to have killed over fifty thousand people during that time. Even livestock were not safe: when cows were fed the infected grains, they lost their hooves, tails, and even their ears before they died.

The relationship between these strange behaviors and ergot infestation had only just been discovered in Europe when the Salem witch trials began, but it is unlikely that news of this breakthrough would have reached the colonies. Eventually nineteen people went to the gallows for the crime of casting spells on the girls. They protested their innocence all the way.

If only someone had thought to question the town baker. Judging from weather records, crop reports, the girls' symptoms, and the fact that the hysteria stopped almost as abruptly as it started, it is entirely possible that the whole event was caused by an outbreak of ergot brought on by an unusually wet winter.

Outbreaks of ergotism are rare today, but a few did occur in the twentieth century. There are still no ergot-resistant strains of ryegrass, but rye farmers now rinse their crop in a salt solution to kill the fungus.

Meet the Relatives

There are over fifty ergot species, each favoring a particular kind of grass or cereal crop.

FATAL FUNGUS

In 2001, a group of medical researchers reopened an ancient murder case. Claudius, emperor of Rome from 41 to 54 BC, died under mysterious circumstances after several months of bitter fighting with his fourth wife, Agrippina. A modern-day review of his symptoms pointed to poisoning by muscarine, a toxin found in several species of deadly mushrooms. But who fed him this final meal? One expert at the conference suggested that "Claudius died of *de una uxore nimia,* or one too many wives."

Another infamous mushroom poisoning case took place in Paris in 1918. Henri Girard was an insurance broker who had some training as a chemist. That turned out to be a good combination for a serial killer: he took out insurance policies on his victims and then killed them using poisons that he obtained from drug wholesalers or mixed in his own laboratory. His poison of choice was a culture of typhoid bacteria, but for his last murder victim, Madame Monin, he prepared a little dish of poisonous mushrooms. She left his house and collapsed on the sidewalk. The authorities eventually caught up with him, but he died before he could go to trial.

Although mushrooms are not truly plants — they're fungi — they deserve some mention for the number of deaths they cause. In 1909, the *London Globe* reported that as many as ten thousand people in Europe died of mushroom poisoning every year. There are few reliable sources today of the number of deaths by mushrooms worldwide, but in the United States, poison control centers get over seven thousand calls a year. In 2005, they reported six deaths from mushroom poisoning. Sporadic outbreaks can kill many more. For example, in 1996, mushrooms killed over a hundred people in Ukraine thanks to an unusually abundant crop in the forest.

Some species contain more toxins than others, but the most dangerous varieties go to work on the liver or kidneys, causing irreversible damage or death.

DEATH CAP
Amanita phalloides

These pale, medium-sized mushrooms found throughout North America and Europe are responsible for an estimated 90 percent of mushroom-related fatalities worldwide. They look similar to the edible paddy straw mushroom popular in Asia, but it takes only about half of a death cap mushroom to kill an adult. The mushroom causes permanent damage to the kidneys and liver, and some victims require liver transplants to survive the ordeal.

A closely related species is the death angel mushroom (*Amanita verna* or *A. virosa*), which is regarded as the most poisonous species. Symptoms may not appear for several hours, which could result in delayed treatment with tragic consequences.

CORTINARIUS
Cortinarius spp.

These small, brown mushrooms resemble shiitakes and other edible species but are highly poisonous. The symptoms may be delayed for several days, making it more difficult for doctors to identify and treat. Cortinarius mushrooms can cause seizures, severe pain, and kidney failure.

FALSE MOREL
Gyromitra esculenta

Found throughout North America, this mushroom looks like the delicious, highly sought-after edible morel mushroom. As with most mushroom poisonings, symptoms include nausea, dizziness, and eventual coma, and death is often caused by kidney or liver damage.

FLY MUSHROOM
Amanita muscaria

Reddish orange with white spots, this is one of the most widely recognized mushrooms in the world and is often used in illustrations of fairy tales. The hookah-smoking caterpillar that sat on a mushroom in *Alice's Adventures in Wonderland* might have been sitting on mushroom like this one. In fact, the symptoms Alice experienced after she nibbled a bit of the mushroom are not too different from the kind of hallucinations that mark the first signs of poisoning from this species. Dizziness, delirium, and intoxication are sometimes followed by a deep sleep or a coma.

MAGIC MUSHROOM *Psilocybe* spp.

Psylocybin and psilocin are hallucinogenic compounds found in different species of mushrooms, but primarily those in the *Psilocybe* genus. The two compounds are listed as Schedule I controlled substances (defined as having no medical use) by the U.S. Drug Enforcement Administration; however, the agency does not list any particular mushroom species on its schedule.

Psylocybin mushrooms are usually eaten or made into a tea; in addition to hallucinations, the effects may include nausea and vomiting, weakness, and drowsiness. Large doses can bring on panic attacks and psychosis. It grows wild throughout the southern and western United States and ranges from Mexico to Canada. Some species are found in Europe as well. It is easy to confuse psilocybin mushrooms with highly poisonous look-alikes, and people have died from eating the wrong species.

INKY CAP *Coprinus atramentarius*

This small white mushroom with a bell-shaped cap is known for its ability to turn as black as ink as it matures. Its poison is particularly devious: victims are only harmed if they eat the mushroom in combination with alcohol. People may experience sweating, nausea, dizziness, and difficulty breathing for a few hours. Most recover, but those who have been poisoned must avoid alcohol for at least a week. Some people experience no harmful effects at all, making this a risky and unpredictable mushroom to experiment with.

Habanero Chile

CAPSICUM CHINENSE

Imagine: a pepper so hot that popping one in your mouth could send you to the hospital. At first, your eyes will water and your throat will burn; then you'll start to have trouble swallowing. Your hands and face will go numb. If you're particularly unlucky, you'll go into respiratory distress—all over one fiery habanero pepper.

In the early 1900s chemist Wilbur Scoville developed a test for measuring the heat intensity in chile peppers. A pepper extract is dissolved in water and tasted by a panel of people who do not regularly eat hot peppers and are therefore more sensitive to the taste. The pepper's Scoville rating is expressed as the ratio of water to pepper extract required to completely quench the fiery flavor. A bell pepper, which contains no heat, would get a rating of 0 SHU, or Scoville heat units. A jalapeño pepper—generally considered to be the hottest pepper any sane person would attempt to chew and swallow—gets a rating of around 5,000 SHU.

If it takes five thousand units of water to dilute the heat in

FAMILY:
Solanaceae

HABITAT:
Tropical climates; needs heat and regular water

NATIVE TO:
Central and South America

COMMON NAMES:
Habanero

one unit of jalapeño extract, what does it take to render harmless a habanero? Anywhere from one hundred thousand to one million units of water, depending on the cultivar and the growing conditions.

The heat levels approached 1 million Scoville units. As a comparison, the pepper spray used by police officers clocks in at 2 to 5 million units.

Just a handful of peppers vie for the title of world's hottest, and they are all varieties of *Capsicum chinense,* commonly called the habanero. The small orange Scotch bonnet variety lends its unique flavor to Jamaican dishes. Another strain, 'Red Savina', earned a Guinness World Record in 1994 for the hottest pepper, with a Scoville rating of over 500,000 SHU. But the hottest habanero in the world may come from Dorset, England, an area not known for its spicy cuisine.

An English market gardener developed 'Dorset Naga' from the seeds of a Bangladeshi pepper. The best seedlings were selected and grown, and after a few successive generations they had a pepper so hot that it could hardly be used as a flavoring. You could hold the pepper by the stalk and rub it against your food, but to do more than that would be to tempt fate. Two American laboratories tested the peppers using a new technology, high-pressure liquid chromatography. The heat levels approached 1 million SHU. As a comparison, the pepper spray used by police officers clocks in at 2 million to 5 million SHU.

Strangely, the active ingredient in hot peppers, capsaicin,

does not actually burn. It stimulates nerve endings to send a signal to the brain that mimics a burning sensation. Capsaicin does not dissolve in water, so grabbing for the water jug to put out the fire in your mouth is useless. However, it will bind to a fat like butter, milk, or cheese. A good stiff drink is also in order, as the alcohol works as a solvent.

But nothing could protect you against the power of Blair's 16 Million Reserve, a so-called pharmaceutical grade hot sauce made of pure capsaicin extract. A tiny one-milliliter bottle of the clear potion sells for $199 and comes with a warning that it must be used "for experimental/display purposes only" and never as a flavoring for food.

Meet the Relatives

Peppers are another notorious member of the nightshade family, which includes tomatoes, potatoes, and eggplant, along with such evildoers as tobacco, datura, and henbane.

Henbane

HYOSCYAMUS NIGER

The particular bit of vegetable wickedness known as henbane was, according to legend, a key ingredient in witches' flying potions. A salve of henbane, belladonna, mandrake, and a few other deadly plants, applied to the skin, would make anyone feel as if they were flying. Mixtures like this have been called the devil's own recipe for good reason. In Turkey children play a game in which they eat various parts of certain plants. A medical study showed that a quarter of the children who played that game became severely intoxicated after eating henbane. Five went into a coma and two died.

Hyoscyamus niger is a weedy annual or biennial that grows to just one or two feet tall and produces yellow flowers, with what have been described as "lurid purple veins." The small, oval seeds are a dull yellow color and are every bit as poisonous as the rest of the plant.

Although henbane contains alkaloids similar to those found in its close relatives, datura and belladonna, it is particularly known

FAMILY:
Solanaceae

HABITAT:
Widespread across temperate climates

NATIVE TO:
Mediterranean Europe, North Africa

COMMON NAMES:
Hog's bean, fetid nightshade, stinking Roger. Henbane means literally "killer of hens."

for its rank odor. Pliny the Elder wrote that the various strains of henbane "trouble the braine, and put men beside their right wits; beside that, they breed dizziness of the head." In fact, staff at the Alnwick Poison Garden in northern England report that two guests have fainted on hot days in the presence of henbane. Was it the heat or the soporific effects of the plant? No one knows for sure, but they warn guests to give this plant a wide berth.

In the Middle Ages henbane was added to beer to enhance its intoxicating effects. To keep this and other suspicious ingredients out of beer, Germany's 1516 Bavarian Purity Law mandated that beer be brewed with nothing more than hops, barley, and water. (Yeast was allowed later after its role was better understood.)

Henbane was used as a very risky form of anesthesia from Roman times until the introduction of ether and chloroform in the nineteenth century. A "sopoforific sponge" would be soaked in the juices of henbane, opium poppy, and mandrake. It could be dried, stored, and later wetted with hot water for some unlucky surgical candidate to inhale. With any luck, the patient drifted into a twilight sleep and awoke later with no memory of the procedure. However, the quality of these potions was very uneven. Too little and the patient would feel everything; too much and they might never feel anything again.

Meet the Relatives   Other *Hyoscyamus* species like *H. albus*, called white henbane or Russian henbane, and *H. muticus*, known as Egyptian henbane, are just as poisonous.

THE DEVIL'S BARTENDER

The plant kingdom furnishes an astonishing array of intoxicating ingredients. A well-stocked bar owes its provisions to everyday crops like grapes, potatoes, corn, barley, and rye. But alcoholic beverages used to include far more interesting plant ingredients. Vin Mariani was a potent brew of coca leaves and red wine that was popular in the nineteenth century. Laudanum, a medicine made from alcohol and opium, was not only prescribed by doctors until the early twentieth century but also tipped into brandy for an addictive cocktail. (King George IV favored this drink.) The ancient Greeks wrote about a fermented barley drink called kykeon that would cause psychoactive episodes. Scholars speculate that it was brewed from ergot-infected rye, making it a sort of ancient precursor to LSD.

Consider some of the wicked plants lurking behind the bar today:

ABSINTHE

The flavor—and bad reputation—come from *Artemisia absinthium,* or wormwood. This low-growing, silvery perennial has a bitter, pungent fragrance. Wormwood is one of the many herbs used to flavor absinthe, that pale green, highly alcoholic drink from the nineteenth century that was believed to cause hallucinations and madness. "The Green Fairy" became an essential part of bohemian café life in Paris. Oscar Wilde, Vincent van Gogh, and Henri de Toulouse-Lautrec were all notorious absinthe swillers. The drink was banned throughout Europe and the United States in the early twentieth century as part of the prohibition movement.

Wormwood is one of the many herbs used to flavor absinthe, that pale green drink from the 19th century that was believed to cause hallucinations and madness.

What makes absinthe so wicked? Wormwood contains a potent ingredient called thujone that at high concentrations can cause seizures and death. Recently, however, mass spectrometer analysis has demonstrated that the level of thujone in absinthe is minuscule, and that the beverage's intoxicating effects can only be blamed on the fact that it is a 130-proof spirit, almost twice as alcoholic as gin or vodka.

Absinthe is now legal in the European Union, as long as the level of thujone is below a specific threshold. In the United States any product containing thujone is strictly banned, but new, thujone-free absinthes are permitted.

MEZCAL AND TEQUILA

Made from the heart of the agave plant, whose sharp thorns and highly irritating sap are so forbidding that jailers planted them around Alcatraz to discourage escape attempts. The blue agave, *Agave tequilana,* goes into the popular spirit that bears its name, but Americans are probably more familiar with the century plant, *A. americana.* In spite of their prickly thorns and preference for dry, desert climates, these plants are actually not cacti. They are in the Agavaceae family and are more closely related to hostas, yuccas, and the popular houseplant *Chlorophytum comosum,* or spider plant. The worm in mezcal is the larvae of a moth or weevil that feeds on the plant.

ZUBROWKA

A traditional Polish vodka flavored with a blade of bison grass (*Hierochloe odorata*), also called sweet grass or holy grass. The grass is native to both Europe and North America, and Native Americans have used it for basketry, incense, and medicine. The plant is a natural source of the blood thinner coumarin, which is not permitted as a food additive in the United States, so zubrowka has been banned since 1978. New technology allows the vodka to be distilled without any coumarin so that it can be imported, and the grass still lends a faint vanilla or coconut flavor. In Poland the unadulterated version is often mixed with apple juice for a sweet, cold drink.

MAY WINE

A popular German drink made from steeping leaves of the ground cover sweet woodruff (*Galium odoratum* syn. *Asperula odorata*) in white wine, giving it a sweet, grassy flavor. Ingesting the plant at high doses could bring on dizziness, paralysis, and even coma and death; recipes for home-made May wine recommend picking young leaves in spring before the plant blooms, and using them sparingly. In the United States the plant is not considered a safe food additive except as a flavoring in alcoholic beverages.

AGWA DE BOLIVIA

A new liquor with a green, herbal flavor made with an extract of coca leaf (*Erythroxylum coca*). The drink contains no cocaine, however—the alkaloid is removed during the manufacturing process, much as it is believed to be for the soft drink Coca-Cola. The liquor contains other herbal stimulants, including ginseng (*Panax* spp.) and the extract of the guarana fruit (*Paullinia cupana*).

CANNABIS VODKA

A hempseed-infused vodka made in the Czech Republic. A handful of *Cannabis sativa* seeds float in the bottom of the bottle, but the manu-facturers assure drinkers that it contains nothing but alcohol to get you high—and it doesn't taste like bong water.

SAMBUCA

An anise-flavored Italian liqueur made from elderberries (*Sambucus* spp.), which contain cyanide in their raw form. However, imbibers have nothing to fear but a hangover from the drink itself.

COLA TONIC

A nonalcoholic mixer made from the African kola nut (*Cola* spp.), another original ingredient in Coca-Cola's formula. The nut contains caffeine and is chewed in West African countries as a mild stimulant. It also contains compounds that can cause miscarriage, and one study showed that extracts of the nut could bring on malaria-like symptoms, including weakness and dizziness. Kola nut is considered a safe food additive by the U.S. Food and Drug Administration (FDA), but cola tonic is rarely sold in the United States.

TONIC WATER

The bitter flavor comes from quinine, the extract from the bark of the cinchona tree in South America (*Cinchona* spp.). Quinine is the medication that saved the world from malaria, and its addition to tonic water gave rise to that classic summer drink, the gin and tonic. (This proved to be an easy way for British colonists in India to take a mild dose of their medicine.) The drug is still found in tonic water today, although at lower doses. In fact, the quinine content in tonic water is what gives the beverage its fluorescent glow under ultraviolet light. Quinine is also found in certain brands of vermouth and bitters. Although it is perfectly safe at low doses, an overdose can cause quinism, also known as cinchonism. Symptoms include dizziness, stomach problems, tinnitus, vision problems, and cardiac symptoms. Overdoses of quinine are so risky that the FDA has issued warnings about using the malaria drug for "off label" uses like the treatment of leg cramps. Pilots in the armed forces are advised not to consume tonic water for seventy-two hours before flying, and to avoid drinking more than thirty-six ounces of tonic water per day.

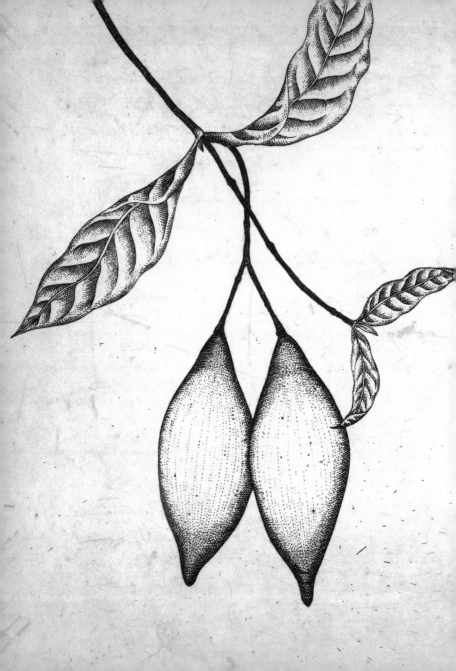

Iboga

TABERNANTHE IBOGA

Iboga is a flowering shrub that reaches about six feet tall in the tropical undergrowth of forests on the central part of Africa's west coast. It produces clusters of small pink, yellow, or white flowers, followed by elongated orange fruit that resemble habanero peppers. The plant contains a powerful alkaloid called ibogaine, which is especially concentrated in the roots and is used to make a controversial medicine that some believe can cure heroin addiction.

Members of the Bwiti religion in West Africa use iboga as a kind of ceremonial sacrament. The hallucinations brought on by the plant are believed to allow members a way to connect with their ancestors, undergo initiation rites, and heal medical or emotional problems. The practice has attracted Western journalists, including explorer Bruce Parry, who made a documentary about his experience for the BBC series *Tribe*. It has also spawned drug tourism fueled by outsiders who want to travel to the African jungle and participate in the ritual, which usually includes a long night of hallucinations and vomiting.

FAMILY:
Apocynaceae

HABITAT:
Tropical forests

NATIVE TO:
West Africa

COMMON NAMES:
Black bugbane, leaf of God

In 1962 a nineteen year-old American named Howard Lotsof got hold of the drug and decided to give it a try. He may have been expecting a recreational drug experience, but he was surprised to find that ibogaine left him with no desire to use heroin, which had been his drug of choice. He invited a few friends to try it, and some of them had similar outcomes. Twenty years later, he was still interested in the ability of this plant to cure people of the addiction brought on by another wicked plant, the opium poppy. He obtained patents for ibogaine-based drugs and founded the Dora Weiner Foundation to support research into alternative treatments for drug addiction. Drug users report varying levels of success with ibogaine therapy. Some believe that the treatment

---

*Iboga has also spawned drug tourism—
outsiders travel to the African jungle and participate
in a ritual, which usually includes a long night
of hallucinations and vomiting.*

---

can "reset" their brain chemistry so that they do not crave drugs and that the hallucinations give them new insights into the underlying reasons for their drug use. However, ibogaine remains a Schedule I controlled substance, and the U.S. Food and Drug Administration has not approved it for any medical use.

There have been several reports of ibogaine-related deaths around the world, including the 2006 death of punk rocker Jason

Sears, lead singer of the band Rich Kids on LSD. He had taken the drug at a detox facility in Tijuana in an attempt to cure his addiction problem.

Meet the Relatives   Same family as the fragrant tropical shrub plumeria, as well as a number of poison plants. Oleander is a relative, as is the poison arrow plant *Acokanthera* and the suicide tree *Cerbera odollam*.

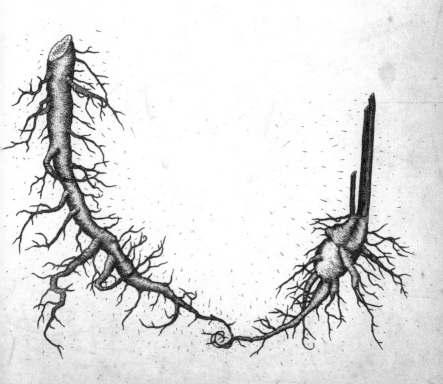

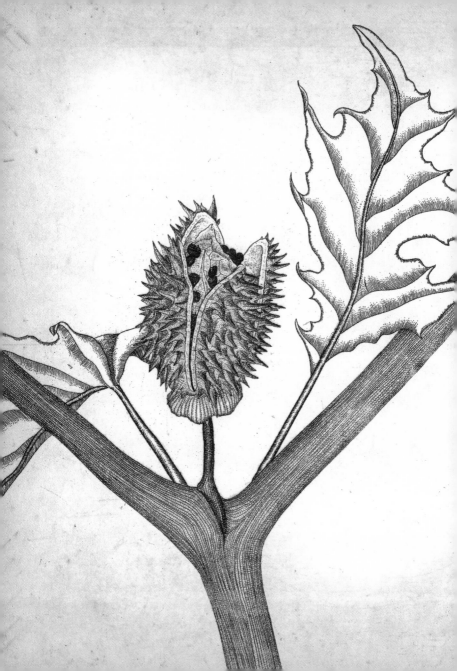

Jimson Weed

DATURA STRAMONIUM

Settlers arriving on Jamestown Island in Virginia in 1607 probably thought they had picked a perfect spot for an outpost. There was excellent visibility to look out for Spanish conquerors, a deep channel to allow ships to navigate, and best of all, there were no Indians on the island. Before long, the ill-fated settlers would find out why.

In addition to the mosquito population, the dirty, brackish drinking water, and the lack of wild game or any other reliable food source, the island was overrun with a seductively beautiful weed. Some made the terrible mistake of trying to add this weed—datura—to their diet. Their gruesome deaths, which were probably marked by delusions, convulsions, and respiratory failure, were not forgotten by the survivors or their children. Some seventy years later, British soldiers arrived to quell one of the first uprisings at the fledgling colony, and the settlers remembered the toxic plant and slipped datura leaves into the soldiers' food.

The British soldiers did not die, but they did go crazy for eleven days, temporarily giving the colonists the upper hand.

FAMILY:
Solanaceae

HABITAT:
Temperate and tropical climates

NATIVE TO:
Central America

COMMON NAMES:
Devil's trumpet, thorn apple, Jamestown weed, moonflower

According to an early historian, "One would blow up a feather in the air; another would dart straws at it with much fury; and another, stark naked, was sitting up in a corner like a monkey, grinning and making mows [grimaces] at them; a fourth would fondly kiss and paw his companions."

It took more than datura to overthrow British rule, but the plant's role earned it the nickname Jamestown weed, and over the centuries that became Jimson weed. The plant, which flourishes throughout most of North America and is common in the Southwest, grows to two or three feet tall and produces striking six-inch-long, white or purple trumpet-shaped flowers that close at night.

> *It took more than datura to overthrow British rule, but the plant's role earned it the nickname Jamestown weed.*

A datura's fruit is about the size of a small egg, pale green, and covered in thorns. In fall, the fruits release a generous handful of highly toxic seeds.

The effects of datura poisoning are similar to those of *Atropa belladona*. All parts of the plant contain tropane alkaloids that cause hallucinations and seizures, but those alkaloids are especially concentrated in the seeds. The levels vary greatly over time and in different parts of the plant, making experimentation dangerous. One recreational user wrote that "the scariest part of this trip was that I stopped breathing automatically and had to make myself breathe with my diaphragm. These conditions lasted all night."

A woman in Canada added datura seeds to hamburger patties, thinking they were a seasoning. (The seedpods had been drying above the stove for next year's garden.) She was in a coma for twenty-four hours before she recovered enough to tell the doctors what she had done. She and her husband spent three days in the hospital.

Teenagers (and adults behaving like teenagers) have made a tea of the leaves in search of a cheap high, but drinking such a tea could be a deadly mistake. Frightening and disturbing hallucinations can come on slowly and last for days. Other common side effects include fevers high enough to kill brain cells and a failure of the autonomic nervous system, which regulates the heartbeat and respiration, leading to coma and death.

Meet the Relatives Members of the nightshade family, all daturas are poisonous. The dramatic bluish purple moonflower, *Datura inoxia*, flourishes throughout the Southwest. Closely related brugmansia is a popular garden specimen.

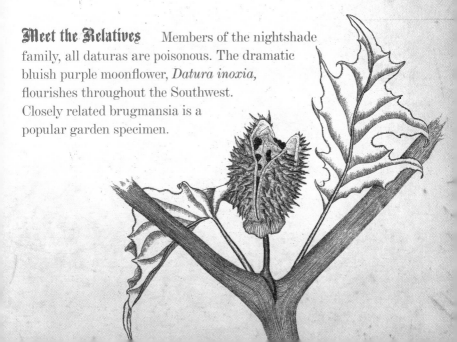

BOTANICAL CRIME FAMILIES

Ever noticed how criminal tendencies tend to run in the family? A few plant families seem to have more than their fair share of black sheep. The characteristics that set them apart—stinging hairs or milky sap or lacy foliage—also give them away.

NIGHTSHADE FAMILY
Solanaceae

Nightshades represent some of the best and worst plants humans have ever encountered. Potatoes, peppers, eggplants, and tomatoes are among the more respectable members of this family. However, when European settlers first encountered tomatoes in the New World, they believed them to be poisonous like the other nightshades they knew. Tomatoes, after all, bear a familial resemblance to their cousin, deadly nightshade, and other dangerous nefarious relatives like the narcotic mandrake, the evil weed tobacco, and the poisonous and intoxicating henbane, belladonna, and datura.

Nightshades have long been viewed with suspicion and distrust. John Smith, a seventeenth-century philosopher, compared the "congealing vapour that ariseth from sin and vice" to the evil powers of "that venemous deadly nightshade, which drives its cold poison into the understandings of men." In fact, many nightshades contain tropane alkaloids that cause hallucinations, seizures, and deadly comas.

The petunia is also a nightshade; in fact, knowing what a petunia flower looks like might just provide a clue for recognizing some other members of this family. Otherwise, an unfamiliar plant that produces small, round fruit and has the general growth habit of a tomato or eggplant should be viewed with some caution.

CASHEW FAMILY
Anacardiaceae

The trees and shrubs in this family typically produce a drupe, a kind of fruit in which the seed is surrounded by a hard pit, which is in turn surrounded by sweet, juicy flesh. (Mangoes are one example, as are the unrelated stone fruits like peaches and cherries.) But what the cashew family does best is produce a toxic resin that brings on painful and long-lasting rashes. And don't light a member of the cashew family on fire—it will produce a noxious smoke that burns the lungs.

Poison ivy, poison oak, and poison sumac are perhaps the most feared members of this family. Mango and cashew trees also produce the irritating resin known as urishol, as does the lacquer tree. In fact, people who are highly sensitive to poison ivy or one of its cousins may experience a cross-sensitivity to mango rind or a lacquer-covered box. Other relatives include the pistachio tree, the ginkgo tree, the poison-wood tree, and the pepper tree.

NETTLE FAMILY   Urticaceae

These small and often harmless-looking plants are best known for that unique anatomical feature, urticating hairs. The fine hairs may look as innocent as peach fuzz, but they often contain a minute dose of poison that is released when the hairs get under the skin. The medical term for painful, itchy hives, urticaria, gets its name from the skin inflammation brought on by stinging nettles.

Most nettles are low-growing plants that superficially resemble herbs like mint or basil, with toothed edges. The Australian stinging tree, widely considered the world's most painful plant, is a member of the nettle family, but the best-known member of this family is the sting-ing nettle, *Urtica dioica*. The hairs are so fine that people unfamiliar with the plant might not even notice them. In addition to the stinging hairs, nettles can also be identified by the small clusters of flowers that emerge from the joint where the leaf connects to the stem. However, the best advice for avoiding the nettle family is to resist the temptation to stroke an unfamiliar fuzzy or hairy leaf.

SPURGE FAMILY   Euphorbiaceae

The highly irritating, milky sap produced by most members of the spurge family sets it apart. Gardeners may recognize the more common euphorbias that are popular in Mediterranean gardens, but other members of this family are not as obviously related: poinsettia, pencil cactus, Texas bull nettle, castor bean, rubber tree, sandbox tree, *mala mujer*, milky mangrove, and manchineel are all spurges. Many of these can burn and scar the skin, but some, like castor bean, also contain powerful poisons that can kill if ingested. At the very least, plants that produce a milky sap should be handled with care, as they may burn skin and eyes. Some spurges can be identified by their colorful bracts; for example, consider the flowers of euphorbias or poinsettias.

CARROT OR PARSLEY FAMILY   Apiaceae

This family conceals some notorious criminals among its otherwise healthy and beautiful members. Carrots, dill, fennel, parsley, anise, lovage, chervil, parsnips, caraway, coriander, angelica, and celery are all plants that a good chef couldn't live without, but even they require some caution: many, including celery, dill, parsley, and parsnips are phototoxic, meaning that skin contact, combined with sun exposure, can cause a rash. One garden flower, bishop's weed (*Ammi majus*), is so phototoxic that exposure to the seeds can permanently darken skin.

But the real danger is posed by relatives like water hemlock, poison hemlock, giant hogweed, and cow parsnip. These wild plants contain neurotoxins and skin irritants, but they so closely resemble their edible cousins that tragic mistakes have been made by hikers and cooks.

Identifying plants in the carrot family is fairly easy. Queen Anne's lace is a typical example; like most members of the family, it produces fine, lacy foliage and flat-topped clusters of flowers called umbels, as well as a carrot-shaped root.

Khat

CATHA EDULIS

Khat played a small but pivotal role in the 1993 battle of Mogadishu in which two American Black Hawk helicopters were shot down. Gun-toting Somalian men stuffed khat leaves into their cheeks and raced around Mogadishu with a jittery high that lasted until late into the night, contributing to the violence and the deaths of American soldiers trapped at the crash site.

Author Mark Bowden found an interesting route into Somalia when he was researching his book *Black Hawk Down:* he flew on a khat plane. Because the leaves must be consumed fresh, Bowden had to pay for the amount of khat he was displacing that day. "What they did was offload two hundred pounds of khat so I could sit on the plane," he said in an interview. "I paid for myself as if I were khat to get into the country."

The leaves deliver a clear-headed euphoria that lasts for hours. In Yemen and Somalia up to three-quarters of adult men use the drug, stuffing a few leaves between their cheek and gum, in much the same way that coca is used in Latin America. And like coca,

FAMILY:
Celastraceae

HABITAT:
Tropical elevations above three thousand feet

NATIVE TO:
Africa

COMMON NAMES:
Qat, kat, chat, Abyssinian tea, miraa, jaad

the khat plant has fueled wars between those who claim it is a benign cultural ritual that has been practiced for centuries and those who see it as a public health menace.

When a khat plane lands in Somalia, its cargo is unloaded and distributed in a matter of hours. Men lounge about in a blissed-out state, chewing their khat, tending to neither their families nor their jobs. Long-term use leads to aggression, delusions, paranoia, and psychosis. But the typical khat user is not deterred by these alarming symptoms. As one man put it, "When I chew it, I feel like my problems disappear. Khat is my brother. It takes care of all things." Another man said, "You open up like a flower when you chew."

Gun-toting Somalian men stuffed khat leaves into their cheeks and raced around Mogadishu with a jittery high that lasted until late into the night.

Catha edulis is a flowering shrub that flourishes in Ethiopia and Kenya, where it enjoys full sun and warm temperatures. The dark, glossy leaves emerge from red stalks, and young leaves may also be fringed in red. The plant reaches twenty feet or more in the wild, but only five or six feet in cultivation.

Its most potent ingredient, cathinone, is classifed in the United States as a Schedule I narcotic, putting it on the same footing as marijuana and peyote. The level of cathinone in the leaves drops sharply just forty-eight hours after harvest, a fact that turns drug smuggling into a wild race. Once the cathinone breaks down, all that is left is cathine, a very mild chemical similar to the diet pill ephedrine. For this reason, police have to move fast to get the plant to a drug lab. After forty-eight hours a major drug bust will become a diet pill raid.

Khat dealers in Seattle, Vancouver, and New York have been busted for selling bundles of leaves under the counter in small grocery stores that cater to Somalian immigrants. In 2006 Somalia's Islamic movement outlawed the plant in the areas it controlled and stopped all flights arriving from Kenya in an attempt to crush the use of the plant. It remains to be seen whether Somalians will give up their drug, which has been called the opium of the people.

Meet the Relatives Khat is related to about thirteen hundred species of tropical and temperate vines and shrubs, including the highly poisonous staff vine, and the equally poisonous spindle shrubs known as *Euonymus*.

Killer Algae

CAULERPA TAXIFOLIA

In 1980 staff working at a zoo in Stuttgart, Germany, noticed an impressive strain of the tropical seaweed *Caulerpa taxifolia* in one of their aquariums. Usually it couldn't handle the colder temperatures that Mediterranean fish require, but this particular specimen was lush, green, and hardy in the cold aquarium. What made it so different? Scientists believe that constant exposure to chemicals and ultraviolet light in the aquarium triggered a genetic mutation that made it particularly tough.

Word got around, and soon the staff at several aquariums wanted to try the plant in their exhibits. Someone brought it to Jacques Cousteau's Oceanographic Museum in Monaco, where it escaped into the wild with just a little extra help. According to one report, in 1984 an employee cleaning the tanks tossed the leftover waste into the sea.

French biology professor Alexandre Meinesz first saw a patch of the algae growing in the Mediterranean Sea near the museum

FAMILY:
Caulerpaceae

HABITAT:
Killer algae thrives in the Mediterranean, along California's Pacific coast, in the oceans off tropical and subtropical Australia, and in saltwater aquariums worldwide.

NATIVE TO:
Originally discovered along the French coast, this algae is native to the Caribbean, east Africa, northern India, and elsewhere.

COMMON NAMES:
Caulerpa, Mediterranean clone

in 1989. He was surprised to see a tropical seaweed growing so vigorously in the cold water, and he warned his colleagues that the plant could become invasive.

The entire plant — its feathery fronds, sturdy stems, and tough rhizoids that anchor it to the ocean floor — is all just one giant cell that can span over two feet in length and grow about half an inch per day.

This set off a decade-long debate over the origin of the plant, the likelihood that it might become invasive, and the responsibility for combating an invasion if it happened. As committees were being formed and papers were being written, the algae made its way to sixty-eight sites around the world, covering twelve thousand acres of the ocean floor.

Today, a lush, green carpet of *C. taxifolia* spans over thirty two thousand acres of oceans around the world, or about fifty square miles.

This is truly remarkable considering the fact that killer algae is a single-celled organism. The entire plant, including its feathery fronds, sturdy stems, and tough rhizoids that anchor it to the ocean floor, are all just one giant cell that can span over two feet in length and grow about half an inch per day. This makes it one of the world's largest — and most dangerous — single-celled organisms.

Killer algae don't kill human beings. The plant gets its nickname from a toxin called caulerpenin that poisons fish. This keeps marine life from nibbling on the plant, which is part of the reason it has spread unchecked in oceans around the world. The lush, green vegetation forms meadows ten feet deep on the ocean floor, choking out all other aquatic life. Fish populations are dying out, and waterways have become clogged with the plant.

This mutant aquarium strain of *C. taxifolia* is exclusively male, suggesting that the entire invasive population around the world stems from just one parent plant. It reproduces only through propagation: a chunk breaks off, gets chopped up in the undercarriage of boats, and then spreads throughout the ocean. The caulerpenin toxin forms a gel that heals the wound within an hour, allowing that fragment to grow and establish a meadow of its own.

Killer algae is classified as a noxious weed in the United States, which means that it cannot be imported into the country or shipped across state lines. It's considered one of the world's hundred worst invaders by the Invasive Species Specialist Group. Attempts to eradicate it haven't met with much success, because chopping up the plant only helps it reproduce. One of the few success stories comes from San Diego, where an eleven-thousand-square-foot patch was destroyed by placing a tarp over it and pumping chlorine into it. Authorities haven't claimed victory just yet: even a one-millimeter chunk of killer algae floating in the ocean could take root and spread again.

Meet the Relatives The edible sea lettuce (*Ulva lactuca*) and other small, green seaweeds are related to the menacing killer algae.

STOP AND SMELL THE RAGWEED

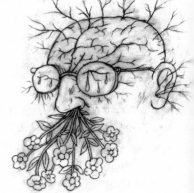

A poisonous seed will only kill you if you chew it and swallow. A painful rash can only spread if you brush up against the leaves. But some plants have figured out how to extend their reach by releasing highly irritating allergens into the air.

There's a reason why seasonal allergies seem to get worse every year. Gardeners and landscapers, in an attempt to be tidy, prefer to plant male trees and shrubs. The females drop fruit, leaving a mess all over the sidewalk or the lawn. But a male tree produces only small, well-behaved flowers—that is, if your definition of *well behaved* includes spewing plant sperm into the air for weeks on end.

In the 1950s and 1960s diseased American elm trees

were replaced with male varieties of wind-pollinated trees. As a result, some cities, particularly in the Southeast, are virtually uninhabitable for people with serious allergies and asthma.

Homeowners are surprisingly reluctant to remove these trees. One allergen expert remembers a family with a huge male mulberry tree in their garden. After blasting the tree with a hose in a misguided attempt to wash off the pollen, both the husband and wife felt their throats close and had to lock themselves in the bathroom all night just to be able to breathe. The pollen had germinated in water, releasing even more allergens than before.

Consider banishing these plants from the yard:

RAGWEED   *Ambrosia* spp.

A versatile weed that flourishes throughout the United States and across Europe. A single plant can produce a billion grains of pollen during a season. The pollen remains airborne for days and can travel several miles, affecting some 75 percent of allergy sufferers and creating cross-allergies with foods that have similar proteins, including cantaloupe, banana, and watermelon. Ragweed releases more pollen when carbon dioxide levels are higher, so global warming will only make the situation worse.

YEW PINE   *Podocarpus macrophyllus*

A shrub or small tree popular as a street tree or as a foundation plant in landscapes, this plant is a heavy pollen producer, and the fact that it is often planted right under windows in suburban landscapes means that allergy sufferers may wake up with a sore throat that will only get sicker if they spend the day in bed.

PEPPER TREE   *Schinus molle* or *S. terebinthefolius*

A controversial landscaping tree that can be invasive and cause a nasty skin rash. The berries are poisonous if eaten. The male trees send copious amounts of pollen into the air over a long blooming season. Because it is related to poison ivy and other members of the toxicodendron genus, people who are especially sensitive to those plants will also suffer around pepper trees. It produces an oil that can vaporize into thin air, causing people to develop asthma, eye inflammation, and other reactions just from being nearby.

OLIVE TREE   *Olea europaea*

Olive pollen is so highly irritating, owing to the number of different allergens it contains, that some cities are trying to banish the tree entirely. The city of Tucson, Arizona, has passed an ordinance banning the sale or planting of olive trees.

MULBERRY   *Morus* spp.

One of the most potent sources of spring allergies, this plant sheds billions of pollen grains that linger on patios and get tracked indoors.

HIMALAYAN CEDAR $\qquad$ *Cedrus deodara*

A fast-growing cedar reaching up to eighty feet tall and forty feet wide, found in gardens and parks throughout mild winter areas in North America and Europe. The small, male cones shed pollen in the fall. Many seasonal allergy sufferers are sensitive to cedar, making this an unbearable tree to be around.

BOTTLEBRUSH $\qquad$ *Callistemon* spp.

A popular, showy shrub in North America, Europe, and Australia. The long, bristlelike red stamens release golden pollen from the tips. The pollen is triangular in shape and lodges in the sinuses, making it a particularly vicious allergen.

JUNIPER $\qquad$ *Juniperus* spp.

This evergreen is a serious but overlooked source of allergens. The males produce cones, along with large quantities of pollen. Some junipers have both male and female organs on one plant (monoecious), which means that they might produce some berries but will also shed pollen.

BERMUDA GRASS $\qquad$ *Cynodon dactylon*

One of the most popular grasses for lawns in the South and warm-weather climates throughout the world, it is also the most allergenic. It blooms steadily, and the flowers often grow so low that lawn mowers miss them. New varieties don't produce any pollen at all, but older varieties are so problematic that some cities in the Southwest have banned them.

Kudzu

PUERÁRIA LOBATA

Kudzu to the rescue!" So proclaimed a 1937 *Washington Post* article about the powers of this exotic vine to control erosion. And indeed, for almost a hundred years the vine enjoyed the enthusiastic support of American gardeners and farmers.

The Centennial Exposition, held in 1876 in Philadelphia, was a carnival of wonders. Roughly ten million Americans were introduced to the telephone, the typewriter, and a miraculous new plant from Japan: kudzu. Plant enthusiasts loved the flowers' fruity, grapelike fragrance and the fact that the vine could scramble over a trellis so quickly.

Soon farmers realized that livestock would eat the vine, making it a useful forage crop. Kudzu gripped the soil and stopped erosion. A government program encouraging the use of the vine gave kudzu all the encouragement it needed.

Kudzu had other plans for the South. The vine made itself at home, growing up to a foot per day during the warm, humid summers. This plant is born to run: Over two dozen stems emerge from a single crown, and each

FAMILY:
Fabaceae

HABITAT:
Warm, humid climates

NATIVE TO:
China; introduced to Japan in the 1700s

COMMON NAMES:
Mile-a-minute vine, the vine that ate the South. To the Japanese, the word *kudzu* means "rubbish," "waste," or "useless scraps."

of those vines can stretch to one hundred feet. A single massive tap root can weigh up to four hundred pounds. Each individual leaf can twist and turn so that it receives the maximum amount of sunlight, making the vine particularly efficient at harnessing the sun's energy and keeping rays from reaching the plants below it.

Kudzu shrugs off cold weather and spreads by underground rhizomes and seeds, which can survive for several years before sprouting. It strangles trees, smothers meadows, undermines buildings, and pulls down power lines. Southerners say they sleep with the windows closed to keep it from sneaking into the bedroom at night.

The vine covers seven million acres in the United States. The damage it has caused is estimated in the hundreds of millions. At the Fort Pickett military base in Virginia, kudzu overwhelmed two hundred acres of training land. Even M1 Abrams battle tanks couldn't penetrate the rampant growth.

But the South has not surrendered. Aggressive herbicide campaigns, controlled burns, and repeated slashing of new growth can keep kudzu in check. Southerners also fight back by eating the vine that is eating them: fried kudzu leaves, kudzu blossom jelly, and kudzu stem salsa all put a bad plant to good use.

Meet the Relatives   Kudzu is a legume; it is related to such useful plants as soybeans, alfalfa, and clover.

LAWN OF DEATH

Who knew grass could be so dangerous? A lawn of wicked grasses could slice your skin with razorlike blades, close your throat with maddening pollen, get you drunk, and poison you with cyanide. One grass even acts as cremator, bursting into flames and sending its seeds and runners over the ashes.

COGON GRASS *Imperata cylindrical*

The bright chartreuse blades grow to four feet tall, crowding out everything in their path. The edge of each blade is embedded with tiny silica crystals as sharp and serrated as the teeth of a saw. Roots can travel more than three feet deep, producing barbed rhizomes that pierce the roots of other plants and shove them out of the way in a sinister quest for world dominance.

Some botanists suspect that cogon grass contains a poison that kills its competition, but poison is hardly necessary: cogon grass's weapon of choice is fire. Thanks to its high flammability, it lures fire into a meadow and sets it loose on the competition, encouraging it to burn hotter and brighter than it otherwise would. (Just one spark from a power saw was enough to turn eight acres in Ocala, Florida, into a conflagration.) Then, like a phoenix rising from the ashes, fresh young cogon blades spring from the charred remains of the roots and grow stronger than ever after the cleansing inferno. When fire isn't available, wind will do, too: one plant disperses thousands of seeds up to three hundred feet away.

Cogon grass found its way here in the 1940s, when the U.S. Department of Agriculture made the perplexing decision to plant it for erosion control and as grazing food for cattle—in spite of the fact that the grass contains little nutrition and was sharp enough to cut the cows' lips and tongues. It thrives in the southern United States but has slowly made its way north.

SOUTHERN CUT GRASS

Leersia hexandra

A swamp-dwelling grass with sharp blades, widespread in the southeastern United States.

PRAIRIE CORDGRASS

Spartina pectinata

Found throughout North America; grows three to seven feet tall with sharp, toothed edges, earning it the charming nickname "ripgut."

PAMPAS GRASS

Cortaderia selloana

Invasive scourge of coastal California. Highly flammable and virtually impossible to kill. Each plant produces millions of seeds. Beautiful feathery plumes are often collected and carried off by naïve tourists, helping spread the seeds even farther.

TIMOTHY GRASS   *Phleum pratense*

A clumping, perennial grass that contains two major allergens responsible for the most severe forms of hay fever; grows throughout North America.

KENTUCKY BLUEGRASS   *Poa pratensis*

A popular choice for lawns and the cause of some of the worst suburban allergies.

JOHNSON GRASS   *Sorghum halepense*

An invasive weed throughout the United States that can reach eight feet tall. Young shoots contain enough cyanide to kill a horse. Death is mercifully swift, usually caused by cardiac arrest or respiratory failure and preceded by only a few hours of anxiety, convulsions, and staggering about.

DARNEL   *Lolium temulentum*

An annual ryegrass that grows alongside cereal crops worldwide. It is often infected by a fungus that if accidentally eaten causes symptoms similar to drunkenness. Two thousand years ago Ovid described a farmer's ruined fields this way: ". . . darnel, thistles, and a crop impure / Of knotted grass along the acres stand / And spread their thriving roots thro' all the land."

Young shoots of Johnson grass contain enough cyanide to kill a horse.

Mala Mujer

CNIDOSCOLUS ANGUSTIDENS

I t sounds like the plot of a horror movie: A group of teenagers went hiking in the Mexican desert and came back with a mysterious rash. The next day, one girl went to the doctor complaining of red, itchy spots on her hand. She was prescribed some antihistamines, which should have done the trick. But the pain only got worse. In a few days, a painful red and purple rash in the exact shape of a handprint appeared on her lower back.

The girl eventually made it to another doctor, who treated her with steroids. The inflammation subsided, leaving patches of brown pigment that faded after a couple of months. But what caused the rash? It appears to have been the work of *mala mujer,* or "bad woman." This desert-dwelling perennial has the toxic sap of a euphorbia and the tiny hypodermic needlelike hairs of a nettle. The victim had probably stumbled into a patch of it on her hike, and her boyfriend must have had remnants of it on his hand when he touched her back.

No one knows how the plant got its name, but perhaps those who had been stung by a wicked woman's wrath recognized the sensation when they encountered *Cnidoscolus angustidens*—often described as one of the most painful plants in the Sonoran

FAMILY:
Euphorbiaceae

HABITAT:
Dry desert environments

NATIVE TO:
Arizona and Mexico

COMMON NAMES:
Bad woman, caribe, spurge, nettle

> *One researcher found the pain from the* mala mujer's *sting to be so excruciating that he called the trichomes "nuclear glass daggers."*

Desert. This perennial shrub grows up to two feet tall and produces small, white flowers; it is easy to recognize because of the distinct white spots on the leaves in the fine hairs covering the entire plant. Although it is not a true nettle, it behaves like one: the fine hairs, or trichomes, easily penetrate the skin and release a tiny dose of their painful poison. One researcher found the pain from the *mala mujer*'s sting to be so excruciating that he called the trichomes "nuclear glass daggers."

According to a 1971 newspaper account, *mala mujer* was rumored to be a treatment for infidelity in Mexico; husbands would brew a batch of it into a tea for their wives in order to control their sexual urges. But wives had a much more potent treatment for men who strayed: a hallucinogenic or possibly fatal tea made from the seeds of a datura.

Meet the Relatives   These other members of *Cnidoscolus* genus are sometimes mistakenly referred to as nettles: Texas bull nettle (*C. texanus*), found throughout the southern United States, and tread-softly (*C. stimulosus*), found in dry scrublands in the Southeast. Both can bring on nausea and stomach cramps, not to mention intolerable pain.

HERE COMES THE SUN

Phototoxic plants harness the power of the sun to do their damage, using sap that burns the skin when exposed to light. In some cases, eating the plant or its fruits makes a person more susceptible to sunburn.

GIANT HOGWEED *Heracleum mantegazzianum*

This weedy, invasive member of the carrot family looks like the older brother of Queen Anne's lace. It's a beefy, sturdy plant that grows over ten feet tall and pushes other plants out of their habitats in streams and meadows. It is also one of the most phototoxic plants you might encounter. One botany textbook shows a round slice of stem placed on a man's arm; within a day, a circular red welt appears, and after three days, it begins to blister. The wound looks disturbingly like the severe burn a car's cigarette lighter would cause.

CELERY
Apium graveolens

Another member of the carrot family, this plant is susceptible to a disease called pink rot fungus (*Sclerotinia sclerotiorum*). The main defense mechanism is to produce more phototoxic compounds to kill off the fungus. Farmworkers and handlers of celery routinely get burns on their skin that show up under sunlight, and people who eat large quantities of celery are at risk as well. One medical journal cited the case of a woman who ate celery root and then went to a tanning booth, ending up with a severe sunburn.

BLISTER BUSH
Peucedanum galbanum

This aptly named plant is also a member of the carrot family; its leaves resemble those of celery. The plants flourish in South Africa; tourists climbing Table Mountain near Cape Town are warned to avoid it. Simply brushing past it can cause a reaction, and hikers who accidentally break off a branch may suffer a severe rash from contact with the sap. The rash doesn't appear for two or three days after contact with the plant and is made much worse by exposure to sunlight. The blisters can last a week or more and may leave brown spots on the skin for years.

LIMES
Citrus aurantifolia, others

Limes and some other citrus fruits contain phototoxic compounds in the oil glands found in the outer rind of the fruit. One medical journal reported on a group of children at a day camp who broke out in unexpected rashes on their hands and arms. Doctors determined that the only children who were affected were those who had gone to a crafts class. They had been using limes to make pomander balls, and piercing the lime peel with scissors spread enough oil on their hands and arms to cause a reaction.

Orange marmalade and other foods containing citrus peel or citrus oil may cause a reaction. Oil of bergamot, a small, pear-shaped citrus, is a popular fragrance ingredient; any citrus-based perfume or lotion could also burn.

MOKIHANA
Melicope anisata syn. *Pelea anisata*

The mokihana blossom is the official flower of the Hawaiian island of Kauai. Tourists are often presented with a lei made of the dark green citruslike mokihana fruit, which are about the size of grapes. The oils are also highly phototoxic: a few years ago, a tourist wore a mokihana lei for about twenty minutes. Within a few hours, a painful, blistering rash appeared on her neck and chest in the precise shape of the lei. It eventually faded on its own, but the marks remained visible for two months.

HERBAL REMEDIES

A number of plants used in herbal teas, potpourris, lotions, or other concoctions can be phototoxic, although symptoms may not show up for a few days. Medical case studies report reactions from Saint-John's-wort, rosemary, marigold, rue, chrysanthemum, fig leaf, and others.

A tourist wore a mokihana lei for about twenty minutes. Within a few hours, a painful, blistering rash appeared on her neck and chest in the precise shape of the lei.

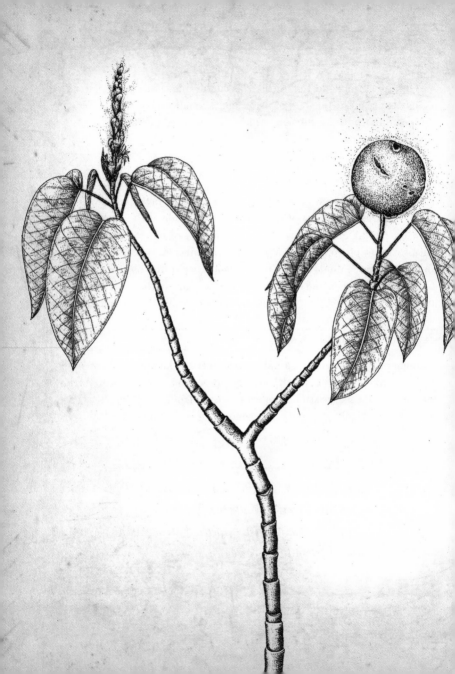

Manchineel Tree

HIPPOMANE MANCINELLA

Tourists vacationing in the Caribbean or on the Central American coast are routinely warned about the hazards of the manchineel tree. As a member of the Euphorbiaceae family, it produces a highly irritating sap that can squirt out of the tree when a twig is snapped off. It also produces a toxic fruit that causes blistering in the mouth and makes the throat swell closed. Even lounging under the trees might be dangerous: rain dripping off them could cause rashes and itching.

FAMILY:
Euphorbiaceae

HABITAT:
Beaches on tropical islands, Florida everglades

NATIVE TO:
Caribbean islands

COMMON NAMES:
Beach apple, manzanillo

The trees are irresistible to tourists. Despite her medical training, a radiologist visiting the island of Tobago was tempted to taste the green fruit that she found lying on the beach. When she took a bite, she found it to be sweet and juicy, like a plum. It took only a few minutes for a burning sensation to start in her mouth. Pretty soon, her throat closed so tightly that she could hardly swallow. The nearest medical remedy, a piña colada, helped a little, but probably only because of the milk it contained.

Captain James Cook encountered the trees on his voyage, and he and his crew also had a nasty encounter with the toxic tree. The men were in need of supplies; Cook ordered them to begin by collecting some fresh water and chopping manchineel wood. Some of the crew members made the mistake of rubbing their eyes, and they were reportedly blinded for two weeks as a result. There's no record of whether they actually burned the wood, but if they had, the smoke would have been particularly noxious.

Even lounging under the trees might be dangerous: rain dripping off them could cause rashes and itching.

The manchineel tree's powers have been exaggerated in art and legend. The tree made its way into the 1865 opera *L'Africaine* by German composer Giacomo Meyerbeer. A heartbroken island queen who is secretly in love with an explorer throws herself under the manchineel tree and draws her last breath, singing:

> *Your gentle perfume, they say, gives a fatal bliss*
> *Which for a moment transports one to heaven*
> *And then brings on the slumber without end.*

Meet the Relatives Part of the Euphorbiaceae or spurge family, which includes a number of other trees and shrubs that produce milky, toxic sap.

DON'T LOOK NOW

Many plants that raise a rash on the skin or produce tiny, irritating thorns can also cause vision problems, including blindness. Here are a few of the most egregious examples:

POISON SUMAC   *Toxicodendron vernix*

Most people in the eastern United States know to avoid poison sumac, a close relative of poison ivy and poison oak. But one young man had to learn his lesson the hard way. In 1836, at the age of fourteen, Frederick Law Olmsted wandered into a patch of poison sumac and got covered in the sap. Soon his face was horribly swollen and he couldn't open his eyes at all.

It took him weeks to make a partial recovery, but the damage to his eyesight persisted. He couldn't return to school for over a year, and he once wrote that the problems with his eyes lasted much later into his life. It may be that this time off was just what the boy needed to nurture his interest in the outdoors and that it led to his career as a visionary landscape designer. He wrote, "While my mates were fitting for college I was allowed to indulge my strong natural propensity for roaming afield and day-dreaming under a tree." Perhaps that year of daydreaming provided the initial inspiration for New York's Central Park, which he designed twenty years later.

TANSY MUSTARD
Descurainia pinnata

This inconspicuous annual grows to two or three feet tall and produces small yellow blooms in the spring. It flourishes in dry fields and deserts throughout the United States. Its bitter taste discourages people from eating it, but cattle will graze on it, and the consequences can be deadly. Their tongues become paralyzed. They begin "head pressing," butting their heads up against some hard object like a fence. Finally, the tansy mustard makes them go blind. Given the head pressing, the tongue paralysis, and the blindness, it is impossible for them to eat or drink, and they die of starvation and dehydration.

MILKY MANGROVE
Excoecaria agallocha

This Australian mangrove tree—another member of the highly irritating Euphorbiaceae family—has earned the common name "blind-your-eye" for the temporary blindness, burning, and itching that its milky sap can cause. If the plants are burned, the smoke will also seriously irritate the eyes.

COWHAGE
Mucuna pruriens

In 1985 a New Jersey couple called an ambulance after developing a severe rash. They blamed it on some mysterious fuzzy bean pods they found in their bed. The paramedics developed the same symptoms, and everyone had to be treated at the emergency room. A nurse at the hospital even started itching after touching one of the patients. The apartment had to be completely decontaminated, including cleaning of all carpets and fabrics. The pods were identified as cowhage.

Cowhage is a climbing tropical vine in the bean and pea family. It produces four-inch-long, light brown, fuzzy pods that are covered with as many as five thousand stinging hairs. Even specimens that have been preserved in museums for decades can cause severe itching. If any of the tiny barbs get in the eyes, they can cause short-term blindness.

FINGER CHERRY   *Rhodomyrtus macrocarpa*

This small Australian tree, also called a native loquat, has long been rumored to cause permanent blindness to people who eat the small red fruits. There were several newspaper accounts of children going blind in the early 1900s, and in 1945 a newspaper reported that twenty-seven soldiers from New Guinea went blind after sampling the fruit. One possible cause is a fungus called *Gloesporium periculosum* that infects the tree. Australians know better than to take their chances.

ANGEL'S TRUMPET   *Brugmansia* spp.

A relative of datura, this South American plant can bring on an alarming case of "gardener's mydriasis," or excessive pupil dilation. Sometimes the pupil enlarges until it almost fills the iris, making it difficult to see. The effect is so frightening that it can send people to the emergency room in fear of a brain aneurysm.

One recent case involved a six-year-old girl who fell out of a wading pool in her backyard. Her parents noticed the dilated pupils and rushed her to the hospital. The doctors asked the parents if the child had been exposed to any poisonous plants, and the parents said no. Later, after a batch of medical tests came back negative, the girl remembered that she had grabbed the plant as she fell out of the pool.

The alkaloids in brugmansia and datura can easily be absorbed through the skin or inadvertently rubbed into the eyes, bringing on these temporary but terrifying vision problems.

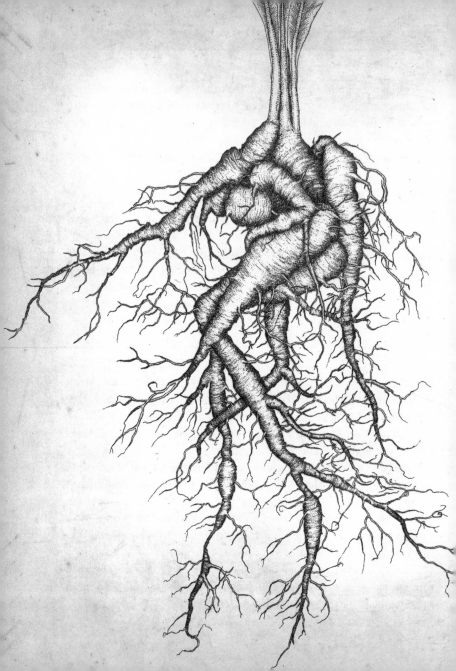

Mandrake

MANDRAGORA OFFICINARUM

Go and catch a falling star
Get with child a mandrake root
Tell me where all past years are,
Or who cleft the devil's foot . . .
—John Donne

Mandrake may not be the worst thug in the night-shade family, but it certainly has the most fearsome reputation. Above-ground, it is an unimposing little plant with a foot-tall rosette of leaves, pale green flowers, and mildly poisonous fruits that resemble small, unripe tomatoes. But the source of the mandrake's power lies underground.

Its long, pointed root can grow three to four feet long and is forked like a carrot grown in rocky soil. Members of ancient civilizations thought that the bifurcated, hairy root looked like a devilish little person, sometimes male, sometimes female. The Romans believed mandrake could cure demonic possession, and the Greeks, thinking it resembled a male sexual organ, used it in love potions. It was also widely believed that the mandrake

FAMILY:
Solanaceae

HABITAT:
Fields; open, sunny areas

NATIVE TO:
Europe

COMMON NAMES:
Satan's apple, mandragora

shrieked when it was pulled from the ground—so loudly that its screams would kill anyone who heard it.

Flavius Josephus, a first-century AD Jewish historian, described one method for surviving the mandrake's horrible screams. A dog would be tied to the base of the plant with a rope and the owner would retreat to a safe distance. When the dog ran away, it would pull the root up. Even if the screams killed the dog, a person could still pick up the root and use it.

> *The friar gave Juliet a mandrake-laced sleeping potion so that she would look "like death when he shuts up the day of life."*

Mandrake was slipped into wine to make a powerful sedative useful for playing nasty tricks on enemies. In a battle over the northern Africa city of Carthage around 200 BC, the general Hannibal waged an early form of chemical warfare by retreating from the city and leaving a feast behind, complete with mandragora, a drugged wine made from the mandrake. The African warriors drank and slept, only to be ambushed and killed when Hannibal's troops returned.

William Shakespeare, perhaps thinking of this event, created a role for the poison in *Romeo and Juliet*. The friar gives Juliet a mandrake-laced sleeping potion and makes this grim promise:

> *The roses in thy lips and cheeks shall fade*
> *To paly ashes, thy eyes' windows fall*
> *Like death when he shuts up the day of life*

Mandrake works its soporific magic through many of the same alkaloids as its deadly nightshade cousins. Atropine, hyoscamine, and scopolamine are all present in the plant and are capable of slowing down the nervous system and inducing a coma.

Recently, an elderly Italian couple arrived at an emergency room, babbling incoherently and hallucinating a few hours after eating the fruit. It took a powerful antidote (ironically, the doctor administered physostigmine, which is derived from the even more toxic Calabar bean), to restore a regular heartbeat and return them to consciousness.

Meet the Relatives

The notorious nightshade family includes peppers, tomatoes, and potatoes, along with deadly nightshade and belladonna.

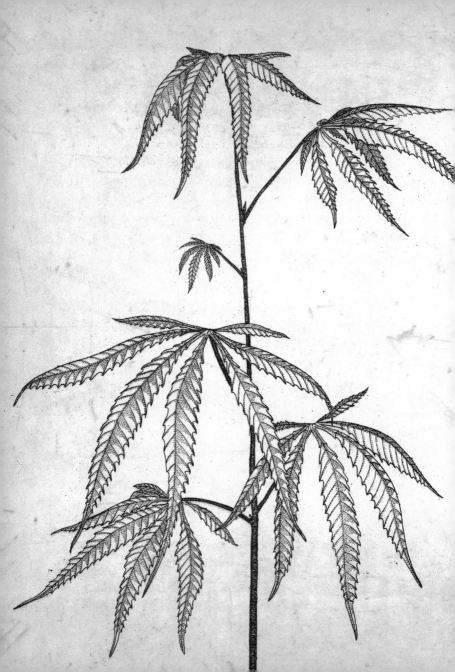

Marijuana

CANNABIS SATIVA

Cannabis has been used by humans for at least five thousand years and regulated or banned for the last seventy. Hemp fibers (from varieties of cannabis that contain very little THC, or tetrahydrocannabinol, and are therefore useless as a drug) have been found in cave dwelling excavations throughout Asia. The Roman physician Dioscorides mentioned the plant's medicinal properties in his medical guide *De materia medica* in AD 70. Its use spread to India, throughout Europe, and eventually to the New World, where early settlers grew it as an economically useful fiber crop. Early drafts of the Declaration of Independence were written on hemp paper. It was used in early patent medications, and even sold in Manhattan as a candy from about 1864 through 1900. "Arabian Gunje of Enchantment," the candy was called. "A most pleasurable and harmless stimulant."

FAMILY:
Cannabaceae

HABITAT:
Sunny, warm, open areas like meadows and fields

NATIVE TO:
Asia

COMMON NAMES:
Pot, ganja, Mary Jane, bud, weed, grass

This weedy, annual plant grows to ten or fifteen feet tall and produces a sticky, intoxicating resin that is also used to produce hashish. All parts of the plant contain THC, the psychoactive compound that brings on a feeling of mild euphoria, relaxation, and the sense that time is passing slowly. Paranoia and anxiety are sometimes experienced at higher doses, but most effects subside within a few hours. Cannabis is not considered to be a lethal plant except to the extent that it may invite automobile accidents, robberies, and electrical fires from indoor grow operations.

The taxonomy of cannabis is still under debate by botanists. Some argue that *Cannabis sativa, C. indica,* and *C. ruderalis* are three separate species, while others believe that *C. sativa* is the only species in the genus, which may have many different strains. Any of these strains or species may be called hemp or marijuana. In addition to the use of hemp fiber for clothing and paper, hemp has also been investigated as a possible biofuel source, and the seeds are used as a food ingredient because they contain protein, healthy fatty acids, and vitamins.

Marijuana was sold in Manhattan as a candy from about 1864 through 1900. "Arabian Gunje of Enchantment," the candy was called.

Some historians suggest that the drive to outlaw cannabis in the early twentieth century came out of the culture wars. Recreational marijuana use was popular among jazz musicians, artists, writers, and other ne'er-do-wells. Its use was regulated, but not banned, by the 1937 Marihuana Tax Act. The beginning of the Beat movement may have been the impetus for finally getting this evil weed out of the hands of America's young people. It was outlawed in 1951 as part of the Boggs Act.

Today marijuana use is banned or strictly regulated in most

countries throughout the world. In spite of that, surveys by the U.S. Department of Health show that 97 million people age twelve and over, or roughly a third of Americans, have used marijuana in their lifetime. Thirty-five million, more than 10 percent of the population, have used it in the last year. The United Nations estimates that nearly 4 percent of the world's population, or 160 million people, consume the drug every year.

Illegal cannabis production is estimated to take up over a half-million acres worldwide and yield forty-two thousand metric tons, making cannabis a roughly $400 billion crop worldwide. U.S. production has been estimated at $35 billion, while the value of the nation's corn crop is $22.6 billion and that of another wicked plant, tobacco, is only $1 billion. In spite of its value as a cash crop, it's also still a weed. The U.S. Drug Enforcement Administration reported that in 2005 law enforcement agencies eradicated 4.2 million cultivated plants and over 218 million "ditchweed" plants, which the agency describes as marijuana plants growing wild that are not typically harvested. (Ditchweed is usually a hemp variety left over from the days of legal hemp cultivation.) That means that 98 percent of the United States' eradication efforts are directed at weeds.

Meet the Relatives Hops (*Humulus lupulus*), used to flavor beer, are in the same family as cannabis. They have no known intoxicating qualities, although the buds may act as a mild sedative. The hackberry (*Celtis* spp.) is a related genus of North American ornamental trees.

Oleander

NERIUM OLEANDER

In AD 77 Pliny the Elder described the oleander as "an evergreen, bearing a strong resemblance to the rose-tree, and throwing out numerous branches from the stem; to beasts of burden, goats, and sheep it is poisonous, but for man it is an antidote against the venom of serpents."

Pliny may have been the most influential botanist of his time, but he was wrong about the oleander. The only relief it would provide a snakebite victim would be a swift and merciful death. This highly toxic shrub is popular in warm climates around the world for its red, pink, yellow, or white blossoms. Because it is so widespread, it has been implicated in a surprising number of murders and accidental deaths over the years. One popular legend is that campers have died after grilling meat over the campfire on skewers made from oleander twigs. This tale is unconfirmed, but the poisons in the sap and bark of oleander could easily contaminate food.

Oleander contains oleandrin, a cardiac glycoside that brings on nausea and vomiting, severe weakness, irregular pulse, and a

FAMILY:
Apocynaceae

HABITAT:
Tropical, subtropical, and temperate climates, usually in dry, sunny locations and dry streambeds

NATIVE TO:
Mediterranean areas

COMMON NAMES:
Rose laurel, be-still tree

decreased heart rate that leads quickly to death. It is also toxic to animals: in spite of the leaves' bitter taste, a cat or dog might be tempted to nibble them. Inhaling the smoke from burning oleander wood can be highly irritating, and even honey made from the plant's nectar can be poisonous. A study of compost made from oleander showed that oleandrin remains in the compost at detectable levels for three hundred days but that vegetables grown in the compost don't absorb the toxins.

A woman in Southern California tried to collect on her husband's life insurance by putting oleander leaves in his food.

Children are particularly at risk because it takes only a few leaves to kill them. In 2000 two toddlers in Southern California were found dead in their cribs after chewing on the leaves. Just a few months later, a woman in Southern California tried to collect on her husband's life insurance by putting the leaves in his food. He went to the hospital with severe gastrointestinal problems, but he survived. As he was recuperating, his wife finished the job by offering him Gatorade laced with antifreeze. She is now one of fifteen women on California's death row, and the only one who attempted murder with a plant.

Oleander-related suicide attempts turn up regularly in medical literature; particularly among nursing-home patients, probably because the plant is popular in landscapes and is well known among elderly people as a poisonous plant. In Sri Lanka a related plant called the yellow oleander (*Thevetia peruviana*) has become the most common method of suicide, particularly among women. Recent studies of the problem sampled over nineteen hundred hospital patients who had poisoned themselves with yellow oleander seeds. Although only about 5 percent of the patients died, the elderly were particularly successful. This may have been due to their frailty, or to their determination, as they tended to ingest more seeds than younger people.

Unfortunately, oleander also has a reputation as a medicinal plant, leading people suffering from certain kinds of cancer or heart problems to attempt an oleander soup or tea from recipes they find online. This practice is very dangerous. Although there have been attempts to market an extract called Anvirzel in the United States, it has not received approval from the U.S. Food and Drug Administration.

Meet the Relatives   Other flowering trees and shrubs in the family include the fragrant plumeria; the highly toxic cerbera; the periwinkle; and yellow oleander, *Thevetia peruviana*.

FORBIDDEN GARDEN

Dangerous plants don't just lurk in Amazon rain forests or tropical jungles. They may be widely available at your local garden center but not labeled as poisonous. When in doubt, ask—and remind children not to nibble anything they haven't already seen at the dinner table. Look no farther than your own backyard for these poisonous beauties:

AZALEA AND RHODODENDRON   *Rhododendron* spp.

A popular group of shrubs containing over eight hundred species and thousands of varieties. The poison grayanotoxin can be found in the leaves, flowers, nectar, and pollen. Eating any part of the plant can cause heart problems, vomiting, dizziness, and extreme weakness. Honey made from rhododendrons can be toxic, too. Pliny the Elder wondered why Nature would allow the creation of toxic honey and wrote around AD 77, "What, in fact, can have been her motive, except to render mankind a little more cautious and somewhat less greedy?"

BLACK LOCUST   *Robina psuedoacacia*

This North American native tree produces clusters of wisteria-like pink, lilac, or cream-colored flowers, but its branches are covered with sharp thorns and all parts of the plant except the flowers are toxic. The toxin, called robin, is similar to ricin and abrin (produced by castor beans and rosary peas, respectively), and although robin is milder, it can cause a weak pulse, stomach upset, headache, and coldness of the extremities. The bark is especially toxic in fall.

COLCHICUM   *Colchicum* spp.

These flowering plants are sometimes called autumn crocus or meadow saffron, but they are neither a true crocus nor the plant from which the spice saffron is derived. The corms produce lovely pink or white flowers in the fall, but all parts of the plant are toxic. They get their poison from the alkaloid colchicine, which causes burning, fever, vomiting, and kidney failure. Colchicum has been used since ancient times as a treatment for gout and was the active ingredient for a common naturopathic medication until a rash of deaths in Oregon in 2007 led to an FDA recall of the drug.

DAPHNE   *Daphne* spp.

Shrubs popular for the tiny clusters of intensely fragrant flowers in winter and early spring when little else is in bloom. Just one or two sprigs will perfume a room. The sap can be irritating to the skin, and all parts of the plant are poisonous. Just a few of the brightly colored berries could kill a child; those who survive may suffer from irritation of the throat, internal bleeding, weakness, and vomiting.

FOXGLOVE *Digitalis* spp.

Low-growing biennials and perennials with breathtaking spires of trumpet-shaped flowers in shades of white, lavender, pink, and yellow. All parts of the plant can irritate the skin and cause severe stomach upset, delirium, tremors, convulsions, headaches, and fatal heart problems if ingested. The plant produces the cardiac glycoside digoxin, which is used to prepare the heart drug digitalis.

HELLEBORE, LENTEN ROSE, OR CHRISTMAS ROSE *Helleborus* spp.

This low-growing perennial produces dramatic, dark green foliage and beautiful five-petaled blossoms in shades of pale green, white, pink, red, and maroon that appear in winter and early spring. All parts of the plant are poisonous. The sap is irritating to the skin, and symptoms of ingestion include burning of the mouth, vomiting, dizziness, nervous-system depression, and convulsions. The plant was once popular as a medicine; one theory about the death of Alexander the Great was that he had been given a medicinal dose of hellebore. The First Sacred War (595–585 BC) is believed by some historians to have been won after a Greek military alliance poisoned the water supply of the city of Kirrha with hellebore. This would have been one of the first instances of chemical warfare in recorded history.

HYDRANGEA *Hydrangea* spp.

A beloved garden shrub prized for its enormous clusters of blue, pink, green, or white flowers, hydrangea contains low levels of cyanide. Although poisonings are rare, the flowers are used as a cake topper, which could lead people to believe it is edible. Symptoms include vomiting, headache, and muscle weakness.

LANTANA
Lantana spp.

A popular, low-growing evergreen perennial that attracts butterflies and blooms all summer long in shades of red, orange, and purple. The berries contain the highest level of toxins while they are still green. If ingested, the berries can cause visual problems, weakness, vomiting, heart problems, and death.

LOBELIA
Lobelia spp.

The *Lobelia* genus contains a number of beloved garden plants, including the compact, brilliant blue *L. erinus,* a bedding annual that spills out of containers; the spiky bright red *L. cardinalis,* which thrives in marshes; and the tropical *L. tupa,* often called devil's tobacco. One species, *L. inflate,* or Indian tobacco, has also earned the names pokeweed and vomitwort. The poisons in lobelia, called lobelamine and lobeline, are similar to nicotine and can cause heart problems, vomiting, tremors, and paralysis if ingested.

YELLOW JESSAMINE OR CAROLINA JESSAMINE
Gelsemium sempervirens

An evergreen vine native to the American Southwest. The bright yellow, trumpet-shaped, fragrant flowers make it a popular climber and groundcover, and it has been adopted as the state flower of South Carolina. All parts of the plant are poisonous. Children have died from mistaking the plant for honeysuckle and sucking the nectar out of the flowers. Both pollen and nectar can be toxic to bees who visit the plant too frequently when no other flowers are available.

Opium Poppy

PAPAVER SOMNIFERUM

The opium poppy is the only Schedule II narcotic (defined as having a high potential for abuse but can still be prescribed) that you can order through a garden catalog, find at a nursery, buy in a floral arrangement, or enjoy in your own flower bed. While possession of opium poppy plants or poppy straw is strictly illegal, most local law enforcement officers will admit that they have bigger problems on their hands than a few pink or purple flowers in Grandma's garden. Only the seeds of this plant are legal to possess, in recognition of the fact that they are a popular food ingredient.

FAMILY:
Papaveraceae

HABITAT:
Temperate climates, sun, rich garden soil

NATIVE TO:
Europe and western Asia

COMMON NAMES:
Breadseed poppy, peony poppy, Turkish poppy, "hens and chicks" poppy

Experienced gardeners have no trouble distinguishing the opium poppy from its non-narcotic cousins. The plant's smooth, bluish green leaves; enormous pink, purple, white, or red petals; and fat blue-green seedpods give it away. When the flesh of freshly harvested seedpods is scored with a knife, a milky sap oozes out. That sap produces opium, which contains morphine, codeine, and other opiates used as painkillers.

Papaver somniferum has been cultivated in the Middle East since about 3400 BC. Homer's *Odyssey* mentions an elixir called

---

Homer's Odyssey *mentions an elixir*
called nepenthe that allowed Helen of Troy
to forget her sorrows; many scholars believe
that nepenthe was opium based.

---

nepenthe that allowed Helen of Troy to forget her sorrows; many scholars believe that nepenthe was an opium-based drink. In 460 BC, Hippocrates championed opium as a painkiller. Records of its use as a recreational drug date back to the Middle Ages.

It was combined with a few other ingredients and distributed as a medication called laudanum in the seventeenth century. Doctors extracted morphine from the plant in the early nineteenth century. But the drug company Bayer introduced the most popular extract in 1898 when it created a much more powerful drug from the poppy. The name it coined for its new product? Heroin. Bayer sold it as a cough syrup for children and adults, but it was only on the market for about ten years. Still, the drug-using crowd caught on and started taking heroin recreationally.

An alarming increase in heroin use led the U.S. government to clamp down, and by 1923 it was banned altogether. However, heroin use only continued to grow, and today 3.5 million Americans report having used the drug at some point in their lifetime. The World Health Organization estimates that at least 9.2 million people use heroin worldwide. Afghanistan produces about 90 percent of the world's opium, but users in the United States primarily get their fix from Colombia and Mexico.

Opium creates a feeling of euphoria but also depresses the respiratory system and can lead to coma and death. It interferes with endorphin receptors in the brain, making it difficult for addicts to make use of the brain's natural painkillers. This is one of the reasons why withdrawal from heroin is so difficult. Addicts who are thrown into jail and forced to go cold turkey will sometimes throw themselves against the bars of their cell for a distraction from the intense muscle pain. Even tea made from the seeds and seed heads can be dangerous because the level of morphine varies widely from plant to plant: in 2003 a seventeen-year-old Californian died from an overdose of "natural" poppy tea.

It would take an annual harvest of at least ten thousand poppy plants to supply the typical heroin user for a year, but there are no exceptions under the law for gardeners who want to grow the flowers. In the mid-1990s, the DEA asked seed companies to stop selling the seed in their catalogs voluntarily, fearing that the availability of the seeds could contribute to domestic heroin production. Most seed companies ignored the request, and the flower continues to be popular among gardeners. The seeds used in baked goods are harmless in small quantities, but eating a couple of poppy seed muffins could cause a positive result on a drug test.

Meet the Relatives   Other poppies include the Oriental poppy, *Papaver orientale;* the Shirley poppy or Flanders field poppy, *P. rhoeas;* and the Iceland poppy, *P. nudicaule.* The orange California poppy is not related; this native wildflower is *Eschscholzia californica.*

DREADFUL BOUQUET

O n July 2, 1881, Charles Julius Guiteau shot President James Garfield. His aim was not quite good enough to kill the president; Garfield lived for eleven weeks as doctors probed his internal organs with unsterilized instruments, searching for the bullet that was actually lodged near his spine. Guiteau tried to use this bit of medical malpractice in his bizarre, theatrical trial, claiming, "The doctors killed Garfield, I just shot him." Nonetheless, he was sentenced to die by hanging.

On the morning of his execution, his sister brought him a bouquet of flowers. Prison officials intercepted the bouquet and later discovered that there was enough arsenic tucked between the petals to kill several men. Although the sister denied having poisoned

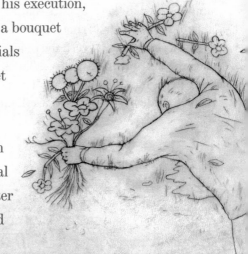

her brother's bouquet, it was well known that Guiteau feared the hangman's noose and would have preferred to die some other way.

Was the arsenic necessary? With a little planning, Guiteau's sister could have put together a bouquet of flowers that would do quite a bit of damage all by themselves.

LARKSPUR AND DELPHINIUM *Consolida ajacis, Delphinium* spp.

Favored by flower lovers for their tall spires of pink, blue, lavender, or white blossoms and their fine, lacy foliage. The plants contain a poison similar to that found in a relative, aconite. The amount of toxins vary according to the species and the age of the plant, but a lethal dose would not be out of the question if someone ate enough of it.

LILY-OF-THE-VALLEY *Convallaria majalis*

A spring-flowering plant with a heavenly fragrance, it contains a few different cardiac glycosides and can cause headache, nausea, cardiac symptoms, and even heart failure at high doses. The red berries the plant produces after it blooms are also toxic.

BLEEDING HEART *Dicentra* spp.

A lovely, old-fashioned flower named for the shape of its blossoms, which resemble a heart with a drop of blood suspended from it. Bleeding hearts contain toxic alkaloids that could cause nausea, seizures, and respiratory problems.

SWEET PEA
Lathyrus odoratus

Resembles a normal pea vine, except that its flowers are larger, more colorful, and incredibly fragrant. All parts are mildly poisonous, but the young shoots and seedpods contain poisonous amino acids called lathyrogens. Sweet pea is one of a number of pea and vetch plants in the genus *Lathyrus* that can cause lathyrism, which brings on paralysis, weakness, and tremors.

TULIP
Tulipa spp.

Produces a highly irritating sap hazardous to horticultural workers. Touching the bulbs can irritate the skin, and workers in Holland's bulb industry know that even the dry dust produced by the bulbs may bring on respiratory problems. A syndrome called tulip finger is an occupational hazard for florists who handle the plants all day. They can experience painful swelling, red rashes, and cracks in the skin.

Tulip bulbs have been mistaken for onions and eaten during times of famine in Holland—a bad idea since a dinner of tulip bulbs would bring on vomiting, breathing problems, and severe weakness.

HYACINTH
Hyacinthus orientalis

Also well known in the flower industry for causing "hyacinth itch" if the bulbs are handled with bare hands. Its sap can also irritate the skin.

ALSTROEMERIA OR PERUVIAN LILY
Alstroemeria spp.

Brings on the same kind of dermatitis as tulips and hyacinths. Cross-sensitivity can develop among these different varieties of flowers, making for a potent combination of painful skin problems.

CHRYSANTHEMUM
Chrysanthemum spp.

Blossoms have been used in teas and for medicinal purposes, but the plants can cause a severe allergic reaction. Some people may develop skin rashes, swollen eyes, and other symptoms. Certain species are used to produce pyrethrum, an organic insecticide.

Prison officials intercepted the bouquet and later discovered that there was enough arsenic tucked between the petals to kill several men.

ACONITE
Aconitum napellus

Aconite, or monkshood, is a popular garden flower that produces spires of blue or white blossoms similar to those of larkspur and delphinium. While they are beautiful in a bouquet, the poison contained in the plant is so deadly that it can paralyze the nerves and even kill. Florists should avoid handling the stems with their bare hands; even skin contact can bring on numbness and cardiac problems.

Peacock Flower

CAESALPINIA PULCHERRIMA
(SYN. POINCIANA PULCHERRIMA)

The peacock flower plays a tragic role in the history of the slave trade. This beautiful tropical shrub, with its fine, lacy leaves and brilliant orange flowers that are irresistible to hummingbirds, produces a seedpod whose poison was well known to women of the West Indies.

Medical literature of the eighteenth century describes the attempts of slave women to end their pregnancies so that their children would not contribute to the wealth of a slave owner. This rebellion took many forms: some women sought medicine from the plantation doctor in the hopes that it would cause a miscarriage, but others relied on plants like the peacock flower. It was believed to help bring on menstruation, or "bring down the flowers," as European doctors sometimes called it.

In 1705 botanical explorer Maria Sibylla Merian first described the ways in which West Indian slaves would use the plant as a form of resistance against their owners: "The Indians, who are not treated well by their Dutch masters, use the

FAMILY:
Fabaceae

HABITAT:
Tropical and subtropical mountain slopes, lowland rain forest

NATIVE TO:
West Indies

COMMON NAMES:
Red bird of paradise, Barbados pride, ayoowiri, flos pavonis, tsjétti mandáru

seeds [of this plant] to abort their children, so that their children will not become slaves like they are. The black slaves from Guinea and Angola have demanded to be well-treated, threatening to refuse to have children. In fact, they sometimes take their own lives because they are treated so badly, and because they believe they will be born again, free and living in their own land. They told me this themselves."

> *"The Indians,*
> *who are not treated well*
> *by their Dutch masters,*
> *use the seeds*
> *[of the peacock flower]*
> *to abort their children,*
> *so that their children*
> *will not become*
> *slaves like they are."*

The peacock flower became a popular ornamental shrub among plant collectors in Europe. It flourishes throughout the southern United States, especially in Florida, Arizona, and California. In areas with mild winters, it can grow to twenty feet tall. The bark is covered with sharp prickles that make it difficult to handle. The red, yellow, or orange flowers bloom all summer, giving way in the fall to flat brown pods that contain the poisonous seeds.

The women of the West Indies hid their secret well: throughout its history as an ornamental shrub, very little has been mentioned in the botanical literature about the role it played in the lives of desperate slave women struggling against the terrible situation they found themselves in.

Meet the Relatives *Caesalpinia* includes about seventy species of tropical shrubs and small trees. *C. gilliesii*, also called bird of paradise shrub, is a popular ornamental in the Southwest. The tannin in its seeds makes it toxic, but most people recover from the poison's severe gastrointestinal effects after twenty-four hours.

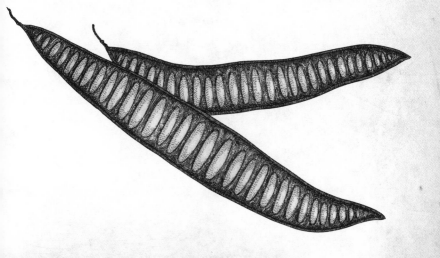

Peyote Cactus

LOPHOPHORA WILLIAMSII

When Spanish missionaries arrived in the New World, they observed the ritual use of the peyote cactus (mescaline) by Native Americans and called it witchcraft. Conquistadores and colonists banned it and drove its use underground. Ironically, when white settlers objected to peyote use, it was usually expressed in terms of the harm it might inflict on Native Americans. This belief continued into the twentieth century. In 1923, the *New York Times* quoted one antipeyote crusader as saying that those who use peyote may be beyond help: "The alcoholic subject may by careful treatment escape physical and mental weakness, but the mescal[ine] fiend travels to absolute incompetency."

This diminutive, slow-growing cactus forms the shape of a button one to two inches across, with no spines. Left to its own devices, a small, white flower blooms on top of the cactus and then goes to seed. But don't go looking for peyote gardens in the desert: overharvesting of the cactus has made the plant scarce in the Southwest.

FAMILY:
Cactaceae

HABITAT:
Desert, but prefers some humidity for seed germination

NATIVE TO:
Southwestern United States and Mexico

COMMON NAMES:
Peyote, buttons, mescaline, challote, devil's root, white mule

The bitter, dried peyote buttons are either eaten or made into a tea. The initial effects can be quite terrifying and include anxiety, dizziness, headache, chills, extreme nausea, and vomiting. The hallucinations that follow have been described as an intense experience of bright colors, increased awareness of sounds, and clarity of thought. However, the experience of peyote intoxication can vary widely and has also been described as "a chemically induced model of mental illness."

Use of the peyote cactus in Native American religious rituals has long been greeted with skepticism in the United States. Dr. Harvey W. Wiley, a tireless advocate for food and drug safety in the early twentieth century, once complained to the Senate Committee on Indian Affairs that if the religious use of peyote is permitted, "we will have an alcohol church and a cocaine church and a tobacco church." In 1990 the Supreme Court ruled in the case of *Employment Division v. Smith* that the First Amendment does not protect Native Americans who wish to use the drug in the practice of their religion. In response, Congress amended the American Indian Religious Freedom Act to allow the use of peyote in Native American religious ceremonies. For everyone else, mescaline is a Schedule I controlled substance, and possession is a felony.

Meet the Relatives   Peyote is a member of the cactus family, which contains two to three thousand species. One relative is *Lophophora diffusa,* which has been shown to contain only traces of mescaline, along with other psychoactive components.

PSYCHEDELIC PLANTS

The U.S. Drug Enforcement Agency is scarcely able to keep up with the public's appetite for mind-altering plants. While some of these plants are not necessarily illegal, they are highly sought after among people looking for a "natural high." Unfortunately, most people are not experts at plant identification and can't be sure what they're taking. Also, the level of active ingredient can vary from plant to plant and may even rise and fall throughout the day as weather conditions change. Here are just a few of the psychedelic plants making their way around the counterculture scene:

DIVINER'S SAGE
Salvia divinorum

A tender perennial sage native to Mexico that resembles many other garden sages. It has gained popularity on the Internet as an easy high. The leaves are smoked or chewed to produce a hallucinogenic effect, but many users report a short and frightening experience that's not worth the effort. Although the plant isn't included on the U.S. Drug Enforcement Administration's (DEA's) list of controlled substances, the agency has identified it as an area of concern. Several states have outlawed it; it's banned on most military bases; and some European countries have banned it as well. Unfortunately, news reports often fail to distinguish between this particular species and the many varieties of salvia that are popular in gardens and have no psychoactive effects.

SAN PEDRO CACTUS
Trichocereus pachanoi, syn. *Echinopsis pachanoi*

A columnar cactus with few spines that grows throughout the Andes mountains, where it's used in tribal ceremonies. Like peyote, the San Pedro cactus contains mescaline, but it's not listed on the DEA's controlled substance schedule. As a result, the plant is widely cultivated, but someone growing it with the intent of producing or distributing mescaline could risk prosecution. Another, less-documented cactus relative is *Echinopsis lageniformis,* called the penis cactus for its anatomically correct shape.

KRATOM
Mitragyna speciosa Korth

A Southeast Asian tree whose leaves are chewed as a stimulant in the same manner as coca or khat. At higher doses it delivers a mild euphoria and possible unpleasant side effects including nausea and constipation.

Though not illegal in the United States, it's been banned in Thailand, Australia, and a few other countries for its addictive qualities.

YOPO   *Anadenanthera peregrine*

A South American tree with long, brown seedpods. The seeds contain a psychoactive compound called bufotenine, which has been used as a snuff in the religious ceremonies of some indigenous tribes. The seeds are taken for their hallucinogenic effects, but they can also trigger seizures. Bufotenine is also secreted by certain species of toads. People actually lick toads in an attempt to get high, an act that could land them in the hospital with convulsions and heart problems.

Bufotenine is listed as a Schedule I controlled substance by the DEA, but yopo seeds (or toads, for that matter) are not specifically identified as illegal. A few clinical studies have shown that people with schizophrenia and a few other mental disorders excrete bufotenine in their urine. Yopo is also rumored to contain dimethyltriptamine, or DMT, the active ingredient in ayahuasca, but tests show no traces of it in the seeds.

MORNING GLORY   *Ipomoea tricolor*

Seeds contain small quantities of lysergic acid amide, which may produce an LSD-like trip if eaten in large quantity. The seeds are popular among teenagers who either chew them or soak them in water to make tea. Recent news reports indicate that many owners of garden centers are unaware of the trend and had been selling the seed packets to teenagers in hopes that young people were starting to show an interest in gardening. Kids who consume the seeds have been hospitalized with dangerously high heart rates and frightening hallucinations.

Poison Hemlock

CONIUM MACULATUM

One day in 1845 a Scottish tailor named Duncan Gow ate a sandwich made with wild greens his children had collected for him. Within a few hours, he was dead. The children had made the fatal mistake of confusing the lacy foliage of parsley with that of poison hemlock. It was the last (and, one suspects, the only) lesson in botany the children ever got from their father, and one they would never forget.

The death that hemlock delivers is, from outward appearances, an easy one. Mr. Gow stumbled about drunkenly, his limbs gradually became paralyzed, and eventually the poison stopped his heart and lungs. The doctor attending the death reported that "the Intellect was perfectly clear until shortly before death."

Hemlock's most famous victim was the Greek philosopher Socrates, who in 399 BC was convicted of corrupting the youth of Athens, among other offenses, and sentenced to death. His student Plato witnessed his death. When the time came, a guard

FAMILY:
Apiaceae

HABITAT:
Fields and pastures throughout the Northern Hemisphere; prefers wet soils and coastal areas

NATIVE TO:
Europe

COMMON NAMES:
Spotted parsley, spotted cowbane, bad-man's oatmeal, poison snakeweed, beaver poison

brought Socrates a drink made from the poison, which he drank calmly. The condemned man walked around his cell until his legs felt heavy; then he lay down on his back. The guard pressed his feet and legs and asked Socrates if he had any feeling left in them; he did not. "And then he touched him," Plato wrote, "and said that when it, the coldness, reaches his heart, he'll be gone." A short while later, Socrates grew quiet and still, and then he was dead.

Poison hemlock, a plant in the carrot family, is so toxic that it is known in Scotland as "deid men's oatmeal."

Hemlock poisoning was not always believed to be so gentle. Nicander, a Roman army doctor who lived from 197 to 130 BC, wrote a prose poem about poisons in which he said: "Take note of the noxious draught which is hemlock, for this drink assuredly looses disaster upon the head bringing the darkness of night: the eyes roll, and men roam the streets with tottering steps and crawling upon their hands; a terrible choking blocks the lower throat and the narrow passage of the windpipe; the extremities grow cold; and in the limbs the stout arteries are contracted; for a short while the victim draws breath like one swooning, and his spirit beholds Hades."

Scholars eventually concluded that Nicander must have been describing another plant, perhaps monkshood or water hemlock. Definitive proof came from John Harley, a British doctor who took small amounts of hemlock experimentally and reported his remarkably different findings in 1869.

"There was a distinct impairment of motor power," he wrote. "I felt, so to speak, that 'the go' was taken out of me." He continued, "The legs felt as if they would soon be too weak to support me . . . The mind remained perfectly clear and calm, and the brain active throughout, but the body seemed heavy, and well-nigh asleep."

Poison hemlock, a plant in the carrot family, is so toxic that it is known in Scotland as "deid men's oatmeal." The young plants emerge in spring, and their finely cut leaves and pointed taproots looking deceptively like those of parsley or carrots. They can reach over eight feet tall in one season, producing delicate flowers that resemble Queen Anne's lace. The stems are hollow and speckled with purple blotches that are sometimes called Socrates' blood. If you're in doubt, crush the leaves and smell them. The odor is enough to deter most animals and has been described as smelling of "parsnips or mice."

Meet the Relatives   Poison hemlock is the bad boy in a family that includes dill, celery, fennel, parsley, and anise, which is poisonous if eaten in large quantities.

Purple Loosestrife

LYTHRUM SALICARIA

Charles Darwin was enamored of loosestrife. In 1862 he wrote to his friend Asa Gray, a noted American botanist, hoping that Gray might have some specimens for him. "For the love of heaven," he wrote, "have a look at some of your species, and if you can get me seed, do . . . Seed! Seed! Seed! I should rather like seed of Mitchella. But oh, Lythrum!" He signed the letter, "Your utterly mad friend, C. Darwin."

Darwin wasn't the only one who was mad about loosestrife. European settlers brought the meadow plant to America, where it quickly established itself. Gardeners and naturalists had a real affection for the tall, vigorous wildflower and its gorgeous spikes of purple blooms. For most of the twentieth century, horticulturalists enthusiastically recommended it for difficult spots in the garden, such as shady areas or beds with poor soil or bad drainage. As late as 1982 garden writers recognized its weedy tendencies but still referred to it as a "handsome rascal," as if to suggest that boys will be boys, and gardeners should love the plant for its aggressive nature.

FAMILY:
Lythraceae

HABITAT:
Temperate meadows and wetlands

NATIVE TO:
Europe

COMMON NAMES:
Purple lythrum, rainbow weed, spiked loosestrife

How wrong they were. Purple loosestrife is surely one of the worst invaders the American landscape has seen. It has marched across forty-seven states and most of Canada, and has also made its way into New Zealand, Australia, and across Asia. The plant easily reaches ten feet tall and five feet wide, and as many as fifty stems can sprout from a single, sturdy perennial tap root. If the rootstock wasn't vigorous enough, a single specimen can produce over 2.5 million seeds in a season. Those seeds can live for twenty years before they sprout.

A single specimen of purple loosestrife can produce over 2.5 million seeds in a season. Those seeds can live for twenty years before they sprout.

Purple loosestrife clogs wetlands and waterways, choking out other plant life and eliminating food sources and habitat for wildlife. An estimated sixteen million acres have been infested with purple loosestrife in the United States alone, and eradication campaigns cost about $45 million per year. The plant is classified as a federal noxious weed and is also illegal to transport or sell in many states. Although other species are sold as noninvasive or sterile alternatives to the dreaded purple loosestrife, native plant experts recommend steering clear of anything labeled *Lythrum*.

Loosestrife is native to Europe but does not cause the same damage there. That fact provided a clue to controlling it in the United States. Chemical sprays, mechanical cultivations, and other controls weren't particularly successful, but then researchers tried importing the same bugs that feed on the plant in Europe. Now a few species of root weevils and leaf-eating beetles have been released as a form of biological control, and it's working. So far, it does not appear that the bugs eat native plants, but introducing one exotic creature to control another always has its risks.

Meet the Relatives
Crape myrtles and cuphea, a genus of shrubs with fuchsialike flowers.

WEEDS OF MASS DESTRUCTION

Some plants just have a way of taking over. They are not above choking the competition, robbing it of food, or even releasing poisonous compounds underground to get it out of the way. These plants are not just invasive; they're homicidal.

HYDRILLA

Hydrilla verticillata

A freshwater aquatic plant that migrated from Asia to Florida in the 1960s. It quickly established itself in lakes and rivers, where it puts down sturdy roots and grows up to an inch a day until it reaches the surface. Some individual plants are twenty-five feet long. Because hydrilla is attracted to sunlight, once the plant reaches the water's surface it will often form a thick mat of vegetation that chokes out aquatic life and makes navigation difficult. Water grows stagnant around a hydrilla infestation, encouraging mosquitoes to breed. It is found in warm, freshwater environments around the United States, and it is almost impossible to eliminate because even the smallest fragment can regenerate. One scientist compared it to herpes. "Once you've got it," he said, "you've got it forever."

DODDER

Cuscuta spp.

The U.S. Department of Agriculture has placed most species of dodder on its federal noxious weeds list. This plant parasite looks like an alien life form that has come to suck the life out of the earth's vegetation, and that's not too far from the truth. The long, seemingly leafless stems grow in otherworldly colors like orange, pink, red, and yellow. (In fact, dodders do have something like leaves, but they are really just tiny, almost invisible scales.) Dodder does a poor job at photosynthesis, which is why it needs to get its nutrition from another plant. In fact, after the seeds germinate, the young shoots only have about a week to find a host plant or they will die. The seedlings grow in the direction of possible host plants. Laboratory tests have proven that dodders will reach in the direction of the scent of the plant, even if there are no plants growing nearby at all, showing that it actually does have an animal-like sense of smell.

Once a dodder finds a host plant, it wraps itself around its victim, injects tiny fungal structures into it, and sucks out the plant's nutrients. A single dodder can invade several plants, feeding on all of them at once and eventually killing them. A field smothered in dodder looks like it has been attacked by Silly String.

PURPLE NUTSEDGE *Cyperus rotundus*

The worst terrestrial weed, according to many experts. Found throughout the world in temperate climates, it spreads quickly, crowding out native plants and invading croplands. Tilling only encourages it by breaking up underground tubers, each of which produces more plants. But what makes purple nutsedge particularly vicious is its ability to release allelopathic compounds into the soil, which actually kill the competition. Gardeners who allow purple nutsedge to go unchecked will find that it not only has taken over but also poisons other plants.

GIANT SALVINIA *Salvinia molesta*

This free-floating aquatic fern can double its population every two days, forming dense mats up to three feet deep on the water's surface. One of the largest infestations was a stunning ninety-six square miles. Giant salvinia is found in freshwater lakes, wetlands, and streams throughout the southern United States. It thrives in nutrient-rich water, so it grows particularly vigorously in water enriched by fertilizer runoff or sewer-treatment plant waste.

STRANGLER FIGS *Ficus aurea*

Known for the decidedly unfriendly habit of wrapping around another tree and strangling it to death. The seeds, which are spread with the help of birds, will often germinate high in the canopy of another tree. Strong, woody roots start wrapping around the host tree and reaching for the ground. Sometimes the roots will completely encircle the tree trunk, and when the tree dies the hollowed-out interior remains, leaving the fig tree in the shape of a giant drinking straw.

Although strangler figs are decidedly creepy, they are generally not considered invasive but are looked upon as an interesting botanical curiosity that has its own niche in the ecosystem.

*Once a dodder finds a host plant,
it wraps itself around its victim, injects tiny
fungal structures into it, and sucks out
the plant's nutrients.*

Ratbane

DICHAPETALUM CYMOSUM
OR D. TOXICARIUM

Several plants produce the deadly poison sodium fluoroacetate, but the best-known sources are a couple of flowering trees in West Africa, *Dichapetalum cymosum* and *D. toxicarium*. Because of the plant's geographic isolation, the trees didn't pose much of a threat until the 1940s, when scientists discovered that they could extract the poison and create a potent chemical for controlling rats and predatory animals like coyotes.

The poison is odorless and tasteless, and only a minute amount is required to kill a mammal. Death comes within a few hours, usually preceded by vomiting, seizures, heart irregularities, and respiratory distress. Survivors may experience permanent damage to vital organs. The poison lingers in the body; if the animal is eaten by another animal, it can poison the rest of the food chain. For this reason, ratbane is sometimes referred to as "the poison that keeps on killing."

Sodium fluoroacetate, which is also called Compound 1080, was used on and off until 1972, when the U.S. Environmental

FAMILY:
Dichapetalaceae

HABITAT:
Tropical and subtropical areas

NATIVE TO:
Africa

COMMON NAMES:
Poison leaf, rat poison plant

Protection Agency (EPA) banned it along with sodium cyanide and strychnine. However, the agency later allowed the U.S. Department of Agriculture to continue using the poison in livestock protection collars. The collars contain fifteen milliliters of Compound 1080, and they can be fitted around the throat of sheep and cattle. When a coyote reaches for the jugular, it will get a toxic dose of this poison instead.

The poison lingers in the body; if the animal is eaten by another animal, it can poison the rest of the food chain. For this reason, ratbane is sometimes referred to as "the poison that keeps on killing."

Use of the chemical for predator management is controversial. Some conservationists argue that strapping such a potent toxin to the necks of livestock could inadvertently result in the poisoning of fish, birds, and water supplies. Aerial spraying in New Zealand to kill invasive rats and possums has prompted outcry from activists who oppose the use of this indiscriminate killer.

The poison attracted attention in 2004, when it was used by a mysterious serial killer to wipe out scores of animals in a São Paulo zoo. No trace of the poison was found in the animals' food or water, which suggested a very sophisticated killer with good access to the animals. Camels, porcupines, chimpanzees, and elephants died while zoo staff scrambled to put in security measures.

Although the poison is banned in Brazil, the killer managed to smuggle it in and cause terrible destruction.

In 2006 a little-noticed notation in the Iraq Study Group's report revealed that one of the chemical stockpiles found by coalition forces contained vials of Compound 1080 manufactured by a company in Oxford, Alabama. How did Saddam Hussein get it and what did he plan to do with it? Representative Peter DeFazio, a Democrat from Oregon, wasn't sure, but he thought that the risk of the substance's getting used as a chemical weapon outweighed its benefits as a form of livestock control. According to news reports, the EPA told him that it would only ban the chemical upon the recommendation of the U.S. Department of Homeland Security, and that department told him that it could not recommend the banning of any particular chemical. He introduced a bill outlawing sodium fluoroacetate, but it died in committee.

Meet the Relatives   Ratbane is related to a few other flowering trees and shrubs found in Africa and South America, including those in the genuses *Tapura* and *Stephanopodium*.

Rosary Pea

ABRUS PRECATORIUS

I n the future, a common tropical plant is to play an important part in forecasting our weather," reported the *Washington Post* in 1908. The plant was *Abrus precatorius,* and Professor Joseph Nowack, Baron de Fridland, of Vienna, was its tireless promoter. The baron planned to set up botanical weather stations around the world, where this mysterious tropical vine would be nurtured and carefully read for weather patterns. If its feathery leaves pointed up, that called for a fine day; if they pointed down, thunderstorms were coming.

Baron Nowack was never able to prove his claims and build his weather stations, but he did manage to call the public's attention to one of the world's deadliest seeds.

The rosary pea vine winds through tropical jungles, wrapping its slender stems around trees and shrubs. The mature plant develops a strong, woody stem for support, allowing the vine to climb ten to fifteen feet. Pale violet flowers appear in small clusters on a stalk, and then the pods emerge, holding within them their shining, poisonous jewels.

FAMILY:
Fabaceae

HABITAT:
Dry soil, low elevations, tropical climates

NATIVE TO:
Tropical Africa and Asia; naturalized in tropical and subtropical regions throughout the world

COMMON NAMES:
Jequirity bean, precatory bean, deadly crab's eye, ruti, Indian licorice, weather plant

Each glossy seed is bright red with one black dot at the hilum, which is the scar left behind where the pea attached to the pod. They are the size and color of a ladybug, making them popular beads for jewelry making.

They are also so toxic that a single seed, chewed well, would kill a person. In fact, punching holes in the hard shells to run a piece of string through the seeds puts a jewelry maker at risk: a finger prick with a needle in the presence of even small quantities of rosary pea dust could be fatal, and inhaling the dust is risky, too.

The poison at work within rosary peas is abrin, which is similar to ricin, found in castor beans. Abrin attaches itself to cell membranes and prevents cells from making protein, which kills them. It can take a few hours or even a few days for symptoms to appear, but when they do, the unfortunate victim will be beset by nausea, vomiting, cramps, disorientation, convulsions, liver failure, and after a few days, death. Unfortunately, the colorful seeds are attractive to small children. As an Indian doctor warned, the rosary pea will "kiss a child to death."

Meet the Relatives   *Abrus melanospermus* and *A. mollis* are reported to have some medicinal uses, particularly for skin wounds and bites, but not enough is known about their toxicity.

THE TERRIBLE TOXICODENDRONS

Poison ivy, poison oak, and poison sumac occupy nearly every state in the Union. But most people don't realize how truly evil toxicodendrons can be.

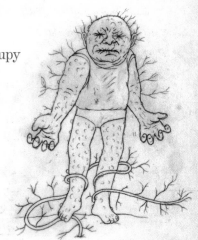

POISON IVY	*Toxicodendron radicans*
POISON OAK	*Toxicodendron diversilobum,* others
POISON SUMAC	*Toxicodendron vernix*

Poison ivy is not, technically, an ivy. Poison oak is not an oak. Poison sumac has nothing to do with sumac trees. And by the way, none of them are poisonous.

The irritating oil they produce, urushiol, is not at all toxic, but it does happen to be an oil that most people are highly allergic to. Oddly

> *Someone who has experienced a severe poison ivy outbreak could be very sensitive to the rind of the mango fruit or other parts of the tree.*

enough, only humans are bothered by exposure to urushiol. No one knows why the plants have singled out people for their unique form of vitriol. Because urushiol creates an allergic reaction—which is nothing more than the immune system gone haywire, fighting some harmless substance, like Don Quixote charging at windmills—each subsequent exposure is worse than the one before. The immune response gets stronger, so that the reaction gets worse with each repeated exposure.

Roughly 15–25 percent of the population is not at all allergic to toxicodendrons and will never develop a reaction. Another small slice of the population could develop a rash but would need prolonged, intimate contact with the plant to bring it on. But unfortunately, about half of all people will break out if they brush up against the plant, and some of them are so allergic that they may require hospitalization. They are called "exquisitely sensitive" by botanists and physicians.

Those sensitive to poison ivy, poison oak, or poison sumac will break out into an oozing, unbearable rash. Since the oils can persist in sleeping bags, on clothing, and in the fur of adorable little dogs, you may not realize that you've been exposed until it's too late. It can take several days for the rash to appear. Once it does, reactions last two to three weeks. Oatmeal baths may be soothing, and the worst cases may require a shot of steroids, but most victims simply wait it out. Fortunately, reactions are not contagious. Those sores will probably get you banished to the couch, but they will not infect the rest of the family.

Even the most common poison ivies and poison oaks are difficult to recognize. Campers can use a simple trick to identify plants containing urishiol: carefully wrap a piece of white paper around the stem or leaf of the plant in question, crushing the plant without coming into contact with it. If the plant contains urishiol, a brown spot will appear quickly on the paper and turn black within a few hours.

If you've had an allergic reaction to poison ivy, oak, or sumac, you're much more likely to have a reaction to some of their relatives, including:

CASHEW TREE   *Anacardium occidentale*

The nuts are only safe to eat if they have been steamed open. The oils in the tree, including the fruit from which the nut dangles (called the cashew "apple"), can cause a breakout that looks just like a poison oak reaction.

MANGO TREE   *Mangifera indica*

Produces a volatile oil everywhere except the inside of the fruit. Someone who has experienced a severe poison ivy outbreak could be very sensitive to the rind of the fruit or other parts of the tree.

LACQUER TREE   *Toxicodendron vernicifluum*

Used for centuries to produce lacquer and varnish, but it is extremely difficult to work with and a real hazard to workers. Even lacquer found in ancient tombs has caused a rash.

Sago Palm

CYCAS SPP.

Gardeners from Florida to California know the sago palm. It is a very tough, slow-growing tree that is widely used as a feature plant in landscapes. The most common variety, *Cycas revoluta,* is a popular houseplant and is often found in botanical garden conservatories. What most people don't realize is that all parts of the plants, especially the leaves and seeds, contain carcinogens and neurotoxins. Pets are routinely poisoned by nibbling on the plant, and it has been responsible for widespread cases of human poisoning as well.

The best-known incident of poisoning occurred in Guam. Locals made a flour from the seeds of the related false sago palm, *C. circinalis.* The traditional method involved leaching the poison out by soaking the seeds in water, but food shortages during World War II may have forced people to eat the seeds without first treating them properly. The poisonous compounds have also been found in bats, which the people of Guam considered a delicacy. The food shortages during the war, combined with the availability of guns when military personnel were stationed there, meant that bats were also hunted and eaten more frequently during that time.

FAMILY:
Cycadaceae

HABITAT:
Tropics, some desert environments

NATIVE TO:
Southeast Asia, Pacific Islands, and Australia

COMMON NAMES:
False sago, fern palm, cycad

Today scientists believe that this caused the mysterious variant of ALS, or amyotrophic lateral sclerosis (also known as Lou Gehrig's disease) that occurred on the island after the war. This peculiar form of ALS included the nerve degeneration common to ALS, the tremors associated with Parkinson's disease, and some symptoms that were similar to Alzheimer's. Medical experts named the syndrome Guam disease and watched helplessly as it became the leading cause of death among native adults living on the island. British veterans and POWs who spent time on the island during the war also had exceptionally high rates of Parkinson's later in life. As the standard of living improved on the island, and people began to eat a more Western-influenced diet, the syndrome all but disappeared.

The American Society for the Prevention of Cruelty to Animals has identified sago palm as one of the most toxic plants that pets may encounter. Just a few seeds can lead to gastrointestinal problems, seizures, permanent liver damage, and death. The palm is especially harmful to dogs that are tempted to nibble leaves and gnaw on its base. In spite of its name, the sago palm is not actually a palm tree. It is a gymnosperm, which means that it produces seed cones similar to those produced by conifers.

Meet the Relatives   Cycas is the only genus in this family. Some are rare and sought after by collectors. These plants are extremely ancient; some show up in the fossil record sixty-five million years ago.

MORE THAN ONE WAY TO SKIN A CAT

Some animals are clever enough to avoid plants that are bad for them, but what are the chances that yours is one of them? A pet bored or confined for long periods of time may be tempted to nibble on one of these common plants. The poison control center for the American Society for the Prevention of Cruelty to Animals gets close to ten thousand calls annually regarding plant poisonings.

In addition to sago palm, any of the following plants may cause a pet owner's favorite symptoms, vomiting and diarrhea, and some are even fatal. Here are some other ill effects:

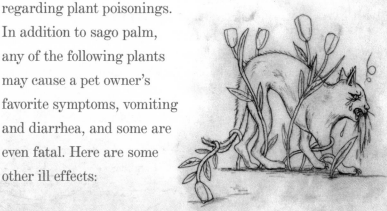

ALOE
Aloe vera

Although useful for treating burns and scrapes, the saponins found in the plant can cause convulsions; paralysis; and severe irritation of the mouth, throat, and digestive tract.

DAFFODIL AND TULIP
Narcissus spp. and *Tulipa* spp.

Bulbs contain a variety of toxins that can cause severe drooling, depression, tremors, and heart problems. The scent of bulb fertilizers, which are made with bonemeal, can prove to be too much for some dogs, who might dig up a newly planted bed and chew on a few bulbs before realizing their terrible mistake.

DIEFFENBACHIA
Dieffenbachia spp.

Common houseplant, also called dumbcane. Contains calcium oxalate crystals that can burn the inside of the mouth, cause drooling and swelling of the tongue, and possibly lead to kidney damage.

KALANCHOE
Kalonchoe blossfeldiana

A small succulent with bright red, yellow, or pink flowers often sold as a blooming indoor plant. It contains a class of cardiac steroids known as bufadienolides that can cause heart damage.

LILIES
Lilium spp.

All parts of lilies are toxic to cats, causing kidney failure and death within twenty-four to forty-eight hours. Think twice before bringing a potted Easter lily into the house, and keep floral arrangements containing lilies well out of reach of your whiskered friends.

MARIJUANA *Cannabis sativa*

Marijuana can depress a pet's nervous system and lead to seizures and comas. If you have to take your stoned pet to the vet for treatment, fess up so the animal gets the right care. Don't worry: vets are used to the "it belonged to my roommate" story.

NANDINA *Nandina domestica*

Also called heavenly bamboo, this ornamental shrub produces cyanide, causing seizures, coma, respiratory failure, and death.

All parts of lilies are toxic to cats, causing kidney failure and death within twenty-four to forty-eight hours.

Stinging Tree

DENDROCNIDE MOROIDES

The diminutive stinging tree has been called the most feared tree in Australia. It reaches about seven feet in height and produces tempting clusters of red fruit that resemble raspberries. Every inch is covered with fine silicon hairs that resemble peach fuzz and contain a virulent neurotoxin. Simply brushing up against the plant results in unbearable pain that may last up to a year. In some cases, the shock of the pain can be so great that it brings on a heart attack.

The hairs themselves are so tiny that they easily penetrate the skin and are almost impossible to pull out. The silicon does not break down in the bloodstream, and the toxin itself is surprisingly strong and stable. In fact, it remains active even in old, dry specimens of the plant. The pain can be reactivated for months afterward by extreme hot or cold, or simply by touching the skin. Even walking through the forest where stinging trees are present can pose a threat. The tree sheds its fine hairs constantly, and passersby run the risk of inhaling them or getting them in the eyes.

A soldier remembers being stung by the tree during his train-

FAMILY:
Urticaceae

HABITAT:
Rain forests, particularly in disturbed areas, in canyons, or on slopes

NATIVE TO:
Australia

COMMON NAMES:
Gympie gympie, moonlighter, stinger, mulberry-leaved stinger

Simply brushing up against a stinging tree plant results in unbearable pain that may last up to a year. In some cases, the shock of the pain can be so great that it brings on a heart attack.

ing in 1941. He fell right into the plant, coming into full body contact with it. He was tied to his hospital bed for three weeks in pure agony. Another officer was stung so badly that he committed suicide to get away from the pain. Humans are not the only ones affected—newspaper accounts from the nineteenth century include reports of horses dying from the sting.

Anyone walking through the Australian rain forest would be well advised to keep an eye out for this plant. It can easily penetrate most kinds of protective clothing. A common treatment is the application of a hair removal wax strip, which will pull out the plant's fine hairs along with your own. Experts recommend a shot of whisky before attempting this treatment.

Meet the Relatives The stinging tree is part of the nettle family; the genus includes *Dendrocnide moroides*, believed to be the most painful. *D. excelsa, D. cordifolia, D. subclausa,* and *D. photinophylla* are also referred to as stinging trees.

MEET THE NETTLES

How much could the tiny, fine hairs on a nettle possibly hurt? Those delicate trichomes act as hypodermic needles, injecting venom under the skin when you brush against them. Urticaria, the medical term for intense, painful hives, gets its name from the Latin word for nettle, *urtica*.

Although any number of painful plants are referred to as nettles, true nettles come from the family Urticaceae. They are mostly weedy perennials that spread by underground rhizomes, and they make themselves at home throughout North America, Europe, Asia, and parts of Africa. A variety of compounds deliver the nettle's sting, including a muscle toxin called

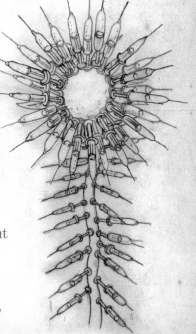

tartaric acid, as well as oxalic acid, which is found in a number of fruits and vegetables and can irritate the stomach. Formic acid, a component of bee and ant stings, is also present in nettles at low levels.

Fortunately, there's a folk remedy for nettle stings: nettle juice. That's right, the sap from the crushed leaves is believed to counteract the acidity of the sting. Dock, a weed that often grows near nettles, may also soothe a nettle sting—and dock leaves are blissfully free of sharp, poisonous spines. There's little evidence about the effectiveness of these remedies, but experts agree that the task of looking for a dock leaf might take one's mind off the pain.

The news on nettles is not all bad: young nettle shoots, when boiled to remove the hairs, are a nutritious spring delicacy, and sufferers of rheumatism have tried deliberately stinging themselves with nettles to relieve their joint pain. There is even a name for this deliberate flogging of oneself with nettles: uritication.

STINGING NETTLE
Urtica dioica

The best-known nettle, growing widely throughout the United States and northern Europe wherever it can find moist soils. A herbaceous perennial, it reaches about three feet in height in summer and dies back to the ground in winter.

DWARF NETTLE
Urtica urens

An annual, low-growing herb considered by some to be the most painful plant in the United States. Also called lesser nettle or burning nettle. Grows in most of Europe and North America.

TREE NETTLE OR ONGAONGA
Urtica ferox

One of New Zealand's most painful plants. Causes rashes, blisters, and intense stings lasting several days. There have been reports that full-body contact with the plant has killed dogs and horses, perhaps from the systemic allergic reaction of anaphylactic shock.

NETTLE TREE
Urera baccifera

Found in South America from Mexico to Brazil. Ethnobotanists have reported that the Shuar of the Ecuadorian Amazon use the stinging leaves to punish their children when they misbehave.

TREE NETTLE
Laportea spp.

Grows in tropical and subtropical regions of Asia and Australia. Unlike most nettles, the sting can last for weeks or months and it can cause breathing trouble. Old, dry branches that have been sitting around for several decades can still do harm.

Strychnine Tree

STRYCHNOS NUX-VOMICA

D r. Thomas Neill Cream was a nineteenth-century serial killer who favored strychnine, which comes from the seed of a fifty-foot-tall tree. Those seeds work well for killing rodents and other household pests—strychnine is also used as rat poison—and Cream discovered that it was effective on tiresome spouses and lovers, too.

He got his start in Canada, where he was forced to marry a woman at gunpoint after she became pregnant. He ran off just after the wedding but later returned to Canada. Shortly after he returned, she died mysteriously. He had an affair in medical school that also ended with the death of the young woman.

Later he set up a practice in Chicago. While he was there, a man died of strychnine poisoning, and the man's wife ratted out Dr. Cream for providing the poison rather than serve time herself.

But that didn't stop him. Ten years later, Cream was out of jail and offering medical services to unfortunate young women in London whose deaths were often blamed on other ailments such as

FAMILY: Loganiaceae

HABITAT: Tropical and subtropical climates; prefers open, sunny areas

NATIVE TO: Southeast Asia

COMMON NAMES: Strychnine, nux-vomica, quaker button, vomit nut

alcoholism. But the true cause of death was the powdered strychnine seed he slipped in their drink. Dr. Cream's pride in his work led him to brag about his accomplishments, and that led to his arrest. By the age of forty-two, he was tried, convicted, and hanged.

Strychnine takes control of the nervous system, flicking on a switch that leads to a flood of painful, unstoppable signals. With nothing to stop the nervous system from firing, every muscle in the body goes into violent spasm, the back arches, breathing becomes impossible, and the victim dies of respiratory failure or sheer exhaustion. Symptoms start within half an hour and death comes a few agonizing hours later. By the end the face of the deceased is fixed in a rigid, terror-stricken grin.

It is rumored to be the sort of poison one could develop a gradual tolerance for. The Greek king Mithridates is believed to have slowly built up a resistance to an entire bouquet of poisons, including strychnine, so that he could survive a sneak attack from an enemy. He tested his potions on prisoners before swallowing them himself; from this legend A. E. Housman wrote these lines:

> They poured strychnine in his cup
> And shook to see him drink it up:
> They shook, they stared as white's their shirt:
> Them it was their poison hurt.
> —I tell the tale that I heard told.
> Mithridates, he died old.

In *The Count of Monte Cristo* Alexandre Dumas writes of brucine, another poison found in the seed of the strychnine tree, and suggests that after taking minute amounts and gradually building up a tolerance, "at the end of a month, when drinking water from the same carafe, you would kill the person who drank with you, without your perceiving, otherwise than from slight inconvenience, that there was any poisonous substance mingled with this water."

Meet the Relatives

Strychnos toxifera bark can be boiled down and used as an arrow poison. *S. potatorum* is used in India to purify water by killing harmful microbes.

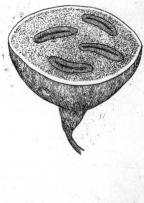

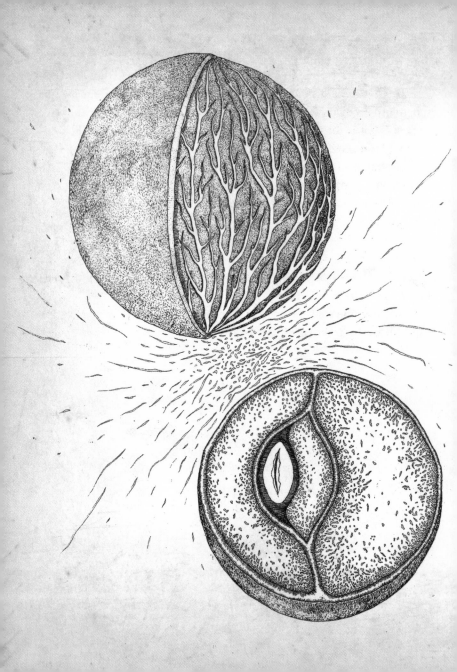

Suicide Tree

CERBERA ODOLLAM

The humid, brackish lagoons of the Kerala backwaters on the southwestern coast of India play host to lion-tailed macaques, Malabar giant squirrels, and a race of small but sturdy goats called Nilgiri tahrs. Here, in the low-lying waterways populated by vipers, pythons, and stinging catfish, grows *Cerbera odollam,* the suicide tree. Its narrow, dark green leaves resemble those of its cousin, the common oleander. Sprays of starry white flowers release a perfume as sweet as jasmine. The fleshy, green fruits are like small, unripe mangoes, except that they conceal a nasty surprise: the seeds' white nut meat contain enough cardiac glycosides to stop the heart within three to six hours.

The advantages of such a powerful natural resource are not lost on the locals. The suicide rate in Kerala is about three times India's average, with about one hundred Keralites attempting suicide, and twenty-five to thirty succeeding, every day. Poisoning is a popular method, preferred by 40 percent

FAMILY:
Apocynaceae

HABITAT:
Mangrove swamps and riverbanks in southern India, as well as southeast Asia

NATIVE TO:
India

COMMON NAMES:
Othalanga maram, kattu aralia, famentana, kisopo, samanta, tangena, pong-pong, buta-buta, nyan

of the despondent. Women in particular favor a dessert of mashed *odollam* nut mixed with jaggery, an unrefined sugar drawn from palm sap, as their final meal. However, the nut's bitter taste is also easily concealed in one of the popular local curries, which are usually served with coconut and rice.

Because the symptoms of *odollam* poisoning resemble that of a heart attack, the seeds have been used as a murder weapon. In 2004 a team of French and Indian scientists conducted liquid chromatography and mass spectrometry analyses to prove that many of those who had died under mysterious circumstances had actually been fed *odollam* by some homicidal acquaintance.

The genus *Cerbera* is named after Cerberus, the hound of Hades from Greek mythology, a vicious three-headed dog with a snake for a tail. He guarded the gates to hell, keeping the dead perpetually trapped inside and preventing the living from entering. But its success as an instrument of suicide is what earned the tree its common name.

"To the best of our knowledge," the scientists analyzing the forensic data wrote, "no plant in the world is responsible for as many deaths by suicide as the *odollam* tree."

Meet the Relatives   *Cerbera* is a cousin of the poisonous oleander. The blossoms of *C. manghas* resemble plumeria. While all the trees and shrubs in the *Cerbera* genus are fragrant and beautiful, they will nonetheless kill you. Even smoke from the burning wood is considered dangerous.

CARNIVORES

Flesh-eating plants know how to make the best out of a bad situation. Many of them live in bogs and wetlands where nutrition is scarce, so they have developed ingenious ways to trap living creatures for their dinner.

BLADDERWORTS *Utricularia* spp.

Tiny plants that live in damp soil and water and suck tiny insects and water into bubblelike traps when their trigger hairs are touched. The traps reset themselves within about thirty minutes, making them extraordinarily voracious plants. Some species of bladderworts are large enough to eat mosquito larvae and tadpoles.

BUTTERWORTS *Pinguicula* spp.

Petite, violetlike flowers belie this plant's carnivorous nature. The leaves exude a slippery ooze that lures fruit flies and gnats to their death.

179

Digestive enzymes excreted by the leaves break down the bodies of the insects, leaving nothing but empty carcasses around the plant.

VENUS FLYTRAPS

Perhaps the most familiar carnivorous plant and easy to grow as a houseplant. Their trap leaves stay open and excrete a sweet nectar that attracts insects. Once a fly wanders inside, the trap springs closed. Glands on the insides of the leaves begin to release digestive juices that drown the doomed bug. It can take over a week for a Venus flytrap to devour its prey, and it may only eat a few bugs in its life. Although people can force a trap to close by running a finger along it, carnivorous plant enthusiasts consider this rude.

PITCHER PLANTS   *Nepenthes* spp., *Sarracenia* spp.

Showiest of all carnivorous plants, growing up to a foot tall and producing gorgeous, otherworldly blooms. Americans will recognize the native Sarraceniaceae family, which includes a number of tall, flutelike, bog-dwelling plants with vivid red and white patterns. Insects wander into the flute of the pitcher plant, attracted to the nectar it produces, and drown in the digestive juices that fill the lower regions of the plant. These are sometimes grown as houseplants; it is possible to perform an autopsy on a well-fed specimen by cutting one trumpet-shaped leaf lengthways, exposing a ghastly mass grave of dead flies.

Plants in the *Nepenthes* genus are also referred to as pitcher plants, but they function a little differently. The plants, which thrive in the jungles of Borneo but are also found throughout Southeast Asia, produce climbing, vinelike stems and cup-shaped flowers that hang from the vine and lure prey. Some of them can hold a quart of digestive fluids.

Nepenthes generally feed upon ants and other small bugs, but they've been known to indulge in a larger meal from time to time. In 2006 visitors to the Jardin Botanique de Lyon in France complained about a nasty smell in the conservatory. The staff investigated, and found a partially digested mouse inside a large specimen of *Nepenthes truncata*.

BIRTHWORTS   *Aristolochia clematitis*

Climbing vines that produce bizarre flowers that vaguely resemble pipes, which is how they got their other common name, Dutchman's pipe. The Greeks looked at the flower and saw something else: a baby emerging from the birth canal. At that time, plants were often used to treat ailments of the body parts they most closely resembled. Birthwort was given to women to help with difficult labor, but the vine is very poisonous and carcinogenic. It certainly would have killed more women than it helped.

Birthwort lures flies with its strong scent and sticky flowers, but it only traps the flies long enough to make sure they get covered with pollen. The sticky hairs wither, freeing the flies so they can go pollinate other plants.

Nepenthes *generally feed upon ants and other small bugs, but they've been known to indulge in a larger meal from time to time.*

Tobacco

NICOTIANA TABACUM

A leaf so toxic that it has taken the lives of ninety million people worldwide; so potent that it can kill through skin contact alone; so addictive that it fueled a war against Native Americans; so powerful that it led to the establishment of slavery in the American South; and so lucrative that it spawned a global industry worth over $300 billion.

This opportunistic little plant contains the alkaloid nicotine that wards off insects. Nicotine has an even more useful function from the plant's perspective: it is so addictive that humans have been persuaded to grow it in mass quantity. Today tobacco occupies 9.8 million acres around the globe and continues to take 5 million lives a year, making it one of the world's most powerful and deadly plants. Some 1.3 billion people around the world hold this plant between their trembling fingers every day.

Nicotiana cultivation began in the Americas and dates back to 5000 BC. There is evidence that Native Americans were smoking the leaves two thousand years ago, but it did not spread to the rest of the world until Europeans discovered the practice when they arrived in America. Within a century, tobacco had migrated

FAMILY:
Solanaceae

HABITAT:
Warm, tropical and subtropical, mild-winter areas

NATIVE TO:
South America

COMMON NAME:
Henbane of Peru

to India, Japan, Africa, China, Europe, and the Middle East. The leaves themselves, and later "tobacco notes" attesting to the quality of a tobacco crop, were used as legal tender in Virginia. America's slave trade was born out of a need for more field hands to bring in a profitable tobacco harvest. People didn't just smoke it; they also believed it could cure migraines, ward off the plague, and ironically, treat coughs and cancer.

But smoking wasn't embraced by everyone, even in the early days. In 1604 King James I called it "loathsome" and said that it was "harmful to the brain, dangerous to the lungs." His statement was proven correct time and again over the next four hundred years, but tobacco use only grew.

Nicotine is such a powerful neurotoxin that it's used as an ingredient in insecticides. Ingesting a leaf is much more harmful than smoking a cigarette because a good deal of the nicotine in cigarettes is destroyed as the cigarette is burned. Nibbling just a few leaves, or making a tea out of the leaves, can quickly bring on stomach cramps, sweating, difficulty breathing, severe weakness, seizures, and death. Prolonged skin contact can also be dangerous: "green tobacco sickness" is an occupational hazard among fieldworkers who must walk through fields of wet tobacco plants in summer.

Nicotine is not the only weapon possessed by plants in this genus. *N. glauca,* or tree tobacco, grows to twenty-five feet tall and is widespread in California and throughout the Southwest. It is notable for the presence of another toxic alkaloid, anabasine. Ingestion of just a few leaves has caused paralysis and death. A man was found dead in a field in Texas several years ago; the cause of death could not be determined until a mass spectrometry analysis showed the tree tobacco's poison in his bloodstream.

In spite of its harmful effects, tobacco continues its death march. Enough cigarettes are produced every year to put a thousand smokes into the hands of every man, woman, and child in the world. Other offerings include snuff, chewing tobacco, and the traditional betel quid, which combines *Nicotiana* with another habit-forming plant, the betel nut. Among some Alaska native tribes, a product called punk ash, or *iqmik,* is popular; it is made by mixing tobacco with the ash of a burned mushroom that grows on birch trees. Some tribal members believe it to be safer than cigarettes because it is a "natural" product, and it is used by pregnant women and given to children and teething babies. However, the level of nicotine is much higher, and the ash helps deliver it straight to the brain, causing some public health officials to describe it as "freebasing nicotine."

In India creamy snuff is popular among women. It is sold in a tube like toothpaste and contains not just tobacco, but also cloves, spearmint, and other tasty ingredients. The manufacturer recommends brushing with it morning and night, and "whenever you need," including when you are "in a state of despair or depressed." They suggest that you "let it linger before rinsing your mouth." One satisfied customer testified that she used it eight to ten times a day.

Meet the Relatives   This evil weed is a member of the nightshade family. Its more toxic relatives include datura, deadly nightshade, and henbane.

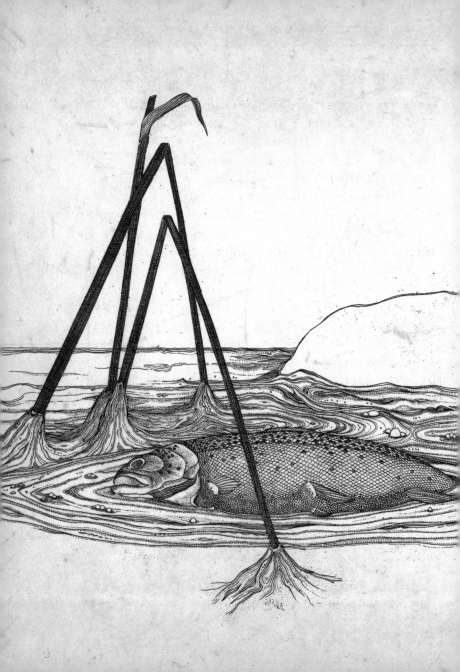

Toxic Blue-Green Algae

CYANOBACTERIA

Pond scum may not technically be a plant—this particular form of algae is actually classified as a bacterium—but this green creature found throughout the world poses a serious threat to humans and animals. Some species of cyanobacteria, otherwise known as toxic blue-green algae, can reproduce or "bloom" suddenly, releasing poisons into the water. People who drink the water or eat contaminated fish have experienced seizures, vomiting, fevers, paralysis, and death.

KINGDOM:
Bacteria

HABITAT:
Saltwater and freshwater environments worldwide, including oceans, rivers, ponds, lakes, and streams

NATIVE TO:
Everywhere; even present in the fossil record from 3.5 billion years ago

COMMON NAME:
Toxic algae

What causes an otherwise normal population of algae to bloom and release their poisons? Scientists are still figuring it out. Fertilizer runoff may play a role, giving the algae something to feed on. Warm temperatures and calm waters encourage the algae to grow, and poisonings do seem to occur more in warm climates during summer months.

Swimming in ponds, lakes, or rivers where algae is visible poses definite health risks. The algae release hepatoxins, which may cause liver failure, and neurotoxins, which may cause paralysis, along with other poisons that cause allergy-like reactions and damage to major organs.

One of the stranger toxins produced by algae is domoic acid. It can bring on gastrointestinal distress, dizziness, and amnesia. Domoic acid poisoning typically occurs when people eat shellfish that have fed off certain species of algae; the syndrome is known as amnesiac shellfish poisoning, or ASP. There is no treatment; so doctors provide whatever relief from symptoms they can and hope that patients recover.

An algae bloom in Brazil killed eighty-eight people and sickened thousands in 1988. Marine biologists in Los Angeles were overwhelmed with sick animals in 2007 when a toxic algae bloom caused sea lions and seals to wash up on the beach in convulsions. Several outbreaks in Australia have sickened people and livestock. But the most notorious incident of all was not understood until recently. In 1961 residents in Santa Cruz, California, awoke to the sound of birds slamming against their homes. Some locals rushed outside with flashlights, only to find dead birds in the street and disoriented, sickened gulls rushing straight at them, attracted by the light.

This story drew the attention of Alfred Hitchcock, who had considered basing a film on a Daphne du Maurier story called "The Birds." Motivated by the real-life incident, Hitchcock got to work on the film. It took more than forty years for scientists to realize that the bizarre behavior of those seagulls was probably caused by a toxic algae bloom that poisoned anchovies the birds ate.

Meet the Relatives There are thousands of species of algae around the world, many of which are quite beneficial to marine life and humans. One of the best-known cyanobacteria is spirulina (*Arthrospira platensis*), a popular health food supplement.

DUCK AND COVER

Any number of otherwise mild-mannered plants can, if provoked, forcibly eject seeds and scatter them at breakneck velocities. If you get one of these plants angry, back away. They could put your eye out— or worse.

SANDBOX TREE   *Hura crepitans*

A tropical tree that thrives in the West Indies and in Central and South America, reaching one hundred feet and sporting giant oval leaves, brilliant red flowers, and sharp spines. The sap is so caustic that it can kill fish or be used as an arrow poison. But you have the most to fear from the fruits, which explode with a loud bang when they are ripe. Its poisonous seeds can fly up to three hundred feet, earning it the nickname "dynamite tree."

GORSE
Ulex europaeus

Flourishes on the English moor, where yellow flowers fill the air with a scent that some compare to custard or coconut. Native to Europe and invasive in some parts of the United States, gorse (also called whin or furze) welcomes fire into its dry branches. The flames cause seedpods to burst open, and rejuvenate the roots. On a hot day, sitting near a gorse can be hazardous: the pods explode without warning, ejecting seeds into the air with a noise that sounds like a gunshot.

SQUIRTING CUCUMBER
Ecballium elaterium

A most unusual vegetable. While it is in the same family as cucumbers, squashes, and other gourds, it's hardly something you'd want to add to your diet: the juice can cause vomiting and diarrhea if you swallow it and sting your skin if you come in contact with it. Its two-inch-long fruits are famous for bursting when ripe, squirting a slimy, mucuslike juice and seeds almost twenty feet away.

RUBBER TREE
Hevea brasiliensis

An Amazon jungle native that made its way to Europe courtesy of enterprising British plant explorers. Although uses for the sticky latex were not immediately apparent, chemists working in the 1800s quickly realized that the substance could be used to erase pencil lines, coat clothing to make them waterproof, and—thanks to some experimentation by an American named Goodyear—could even be used to make tires. In the wild the tree has another trick: its ripe fruits explode in the fall with a loud crack, sending cyanide-laden seeds several yards in all directions.

WITCH HAZEL
Hamamelis virginiana

A beloved North American native that produces star-shaped yellow flowers in late autumn. The extract of the bark and leaves is used as an astringent to treat bites and bruises. The branches have been employed as divining rods to find underground sources of water or mines. In the fall, the dry, brown, acornlike seed capsules snap open and throw seeds up to thirty feet away.

DWARF MISTLETOE
Arceuthobium spp.

A relative of the popular Christmastime mistletoe, is a parasite that sucks the life out of conifers in North America and Europe. Its fruit take over a year and a half to ripen, and when they do, the seeds blast off at the astonishing rate of sixty miles per hour—so fast that you might not even be able to see them fly by.

The rubber tree's ripe fruits
explode in the fall with a loud crack,
sending cyanide-laden seeds
several yards in all directions.

Water Hemlock

CICUTA SPP.

Widely regarded as one of the most dangerous plants in the United States, water hemlock flourishes in ditches, swamps, and meadows across the country, and its flat, umbrella-shaped clusters of white flowers and lacy foliage resemble that of its more edible relatives like coriander, parsnips, and carrots. In fact, most accidental poisonings from water hemlock come about because people mistakenly believe the roots are edible. Unfortunately, the roots have a slightly sweet taste that might encourage someone to take a second bite.

FAMILY:
Apiaceae

HABITAT:
Temperate climates, usually near rivers and wetlands

NATIVE TO:
North America

COMMON NAMES:
Cowbane, wild carrot, snakeweed, poison parsnip, false parsley, children's bane, death-of-man

It only takes a nibble or two to get a lethal dose of the plant's toxin, cicutoxin. It disrupts the central nervous system, and quickly brings on nausea, vomiting, and seizures. One small bite of the plant's root, which is its most toxic part, could kill a child.

In the early 1990s two brothers on a hike mistook the plant for wild ginseng. One man took three bites and was dead within a few hours; the other took only one bite and suffered seizures and delirium but recovered after a trip to the emergency room. In the 1930s a number of children were killed after making whistles or blow darts out of the plant's hollow stems. Children have also mistaken the roots for carrots and gone into convulsions after a few bites.

In the 1930s, a number of children were killed after making whistles or blow darts out of the hollow stems of water hemlock.

There were about a hundred cases of water hemlock fatalities in the United States during the twentieth century, although experts believe the actual number is probably much higher because the victims don't usually survive to report on what they ate.

Water hemlock also poses a threat to pets and livestock. Because the plant's fragrance is not as unpleasant as other poisonous plants, animals are more tempted to graze on it. When mature water hemlock plants are uprooted by tractors, the exposed tap roots can be tempting to hungry animals. Usually the poison works so quickly that animals are near death by the time they're discovered. A single root is toxic enough to kill a sixteen-hundred-pound cow.

The weed grows to seven feet tall and sports purple splotches on the stem. The fleshy roots produce copious amounts of the poison in the form of a thick, yellowish liquid that oozes out when the roots are cut. The most widespread species is *Cicuta maculata*.

In the western United States and Canada, *C. douglasii* thrives in pastures and swamps. It produces unusually thick stems and its flowers are so large and sturdy that they are sometimes picked as cut flowers. This is a very dangerous decorating idea; even a small amount of toxic juice on the hands could find its way into the bloodstream.

Meet the Relatives   Poison hemlock, *Conium maculatum,* which killed Socrates is one relative; others include parsley, carrots, parsnips, and dill.

Water Hyacinth

EICHHORNIA CRASSIPES

This South American native is not hard to recognize. It grows to about three feet tall in water and sports luscious lavender blooms with a distinctive yellow spot on just one of its six petals. Although it is beautiful, the crimes that this aquatic plant has committed are so great that it should be locked away forever—if only that worked.

Water hyacinth forms dense, sprawling mats on the water's surface that even commercial boats can't penetrate. Those mats become islands of their own, providing the perfect environment for other semi-aquatic plants and grasses to sprout. It is freakishly prolific, doubling its population every two weeks. While natural predators kept the plant from taking over its native Amazon, it has gone on a crime spree in Asia, Australia, the Americas, and other parts of Africa. The plant is so horrible that it has earned its own Guinness World Record as the world's worst aquatic weed.

FAMILY:
Pontederiaceae

HABITAT:
Tropical and subtropical lakes and rivers

NATIVE TO:
South America

COMMON NAMES:
Floating water hyacinth, jacinthe d'eau, jacinto de aqua

Its offenses include:

CHOKING WATERWAYS. The plant will quickly take over a lake, pond, or river, slowing the flow of water, sucking up all the oxygen, and strangling native plants.

CLOGGING POWER PLANTS. A vigorous infestation of water hyacinth can shut down a hydroelectric power plant or dam, making the lights go out for thousands of unsuspecting homeowners.

STARVING THE LOCALS. In parts of Africa, fishermen have seen their catches decline by half because of water hyacinth. The people of Papua New Guinea were unable to fish, get to their farms, or go to market because this floating menace stood in their way.

STEALING WATER. Clean drinking water is actually in short supply in some parts of Africa because the greedy water hyacinth slurps it up.

STEALING NUTRIENTS. Although water hyacinth has received cautious praise for its ability to absorb pollutants such as heavy metals, its voracious appetite makes it hard for other tiny water-dwelling creatures to get enough to eat. It devours nitrogen, phosphorus, and other critical plant nutrients until there's nothing left for the others.

BREEDING NASTY PESTS. Water hyacinth can be a breeding ground for mosquitoes, which are a vector for transmission of malaria and West Nile virus. It also provides food and shelter for a particular species of water snail that, in turn, is a particularly friendly host for a few different species of parasitic flatworms. Those flatworms emerge from their snail hosts and swim around until they find a human to infest. The disease, widespread in developing countries, is called schistosomiasis, or snail fever. The little worms travel freely in the body, laying eggs in the brain, around the spinal column, and on any organ that looks inviting. Over one hundred million people are infected worldwide.

The people of Papua New Guinea were unable to fish, get to their farms, or go to market because this floating menace— water hyacinth— stood in their way.

PROVIDING COVER FOR SEA MONSTERS. One report blames water hyacinth for offering convenient hiding places for snakes and crocodiles, giving it an unfair advantage over unsuspecting boaters, bathers, and tourists.

Scientists are looking at the possibility of introducing insects to eat the wicked weed, but they fear they might just be introducing another environmental thug into the mix. Stay tuned—and stay away from water hyacinth.

Meet the Relatives   There are seven different species of water hyacinth, most of which are invasive.

SOCIAL MISFITS

The way some plants behave is disgusting and downright embarrassing. There are the arsonists—plants that use fire as a weapon to clear the way for their offspring and kill off their competition. Some even require a good hot fire for their seeds to germinate. Some cities in drought-prone areas even publish lists of flammable plants to avoid.

Other offenders stink, slobber, and even bleed. Don't invite any of these horticultural misfits to your next garden party.

Pyromaniacs

GAS PLANT OR BURNING BUSH
Dictamnus albus

A flowering perennial native to Europe and parts of Africa. On a hot summer night, the plant produces enough volatile oil that lighting a match nearby can set it on fire.

EUCALYPTUS TREES
Eucalyptus spp.

Native to Australia but naturalized in California; the highly volatile oil produced by the trees helped spread the deadly Oakland fire that killed twenty-five people and destroyed thousands of homes.

PAMPAS GRASS
Cortaderia selloana

A South American native that has become a much-hated invasive plant in the western United States. Each clump can reach over ten feet tall and produce so much dry, brittle biomass that it can accelerate and re-direct wildfires.

On a hot summer night,
the gas plant produces enough
volatile oil that lighting a match
nearby can set it on fire.

CHAMISE *Adenostoma fasciculatum*

A flowering chaparral shrub that produces a flammable resin; the plant is also rejuvenated by fire and is one of the first plants to sprout out of the blackened earth.

Stinkers

CORPSE FLOWER OR TITAN ARUM *Amorphophallus titanium*

Resembles an enormous burgundy calla lily. It usually goes several years without blooming, but when it does, it produces a single flowering stalk that can reach up to ten feet tall and weigh over a hundred pounds. When a corpse flower blooms in a botanical garden, visitors line up to see it, but they are warned to enter the conservatory carefully as the stink can be overpowering.

RAFFLESIA *Rafflesia arnoldii*

Produces the largest single flower in the world at over forty inches across. (The enormous corpse flower is actually a cluster of many small

*The flowers last only a few days
and stink of rotting meat while they bloom,
attracting flies that feed off dead animals
in the Indonesian jungle.*

flowers on a stalk, knocking it out of the running.) This squatty, speck-led, orange plant parasite is truly a flower that only a botanist could love. The flowers last only a few days and stink of rotting meat while they bloom, attracting flies that feed off dead animals in the Indonesian jungle where it lives.

WHITE PLUMED GREVILLEA — *Grevillea leucopteris*

An Australian plant in the protea family that produces gorgeous stalks of yellowish white blooms. Unfortunately, most people won't go near it because of the stink, which is reminiscent of smelly old socks.

STINKING IRIS — *Iris foetidissima*

A lovely English woodland iris whose purple and white blossoms fill the air with the scent of roast beef. Some gardeners believe it more closely resembles burning rubber, garlic, or raw meat gone bad.

STINKING HELLEBORE — *Helleborus foetidus*

Popular in England for its lime green flowers and dark, dramatic foli-age. When crushed, the leaves give off an odor that has been described as "catty" or "skunky" or simply "acrid and unpleasant."

SKUNK CABBAGE — *Symplocarpus foetidus*

Grows in wetlands throughout eastern North America and in parts of Asia. Known for its ability to give off heat; in winter, skunk cabbage can break through frozen ground and melt the snow around it, allowing it to bloom and attract pollinators ahead of spring flowers. Crushed skunk cabbage leaves give off an unpleasant scent similar to a skunk's spray.

VOODOO LILY
Dracunculus vulgaris

Popular among gardeners despite its rotting meat scent. The flowers, which bloom every spring, resemble purplish black calla lilies. The plant grows to three feet tall, making it a striking feature in the garden. Fortunately, the flowers only stink for a few days while they are in full bloom.

STINKING BENJAMIN
Trillium erectum

A lovely red or purple trillium that thrives in moist woodland conditions in eastern North America. This is one of the milder stinking plants—botanists have described it as having a musky scent or smelling like a wet dog.

Just Disgusting

SLOBBER WEED
Pilocarpus pennatifolius

Actually, you're the one who will drool. The 1898 *King's American Dispensatory* reported on the plant's powerful effect on the salivary glands, stating that "the secretion of saliva increases to such an extent as to greatly embarrass speech, the person being often obliged to assume an inclined position that the escape of the saliva may be facilitated. During its salivary action one or two pints of saliva, and even more, may be secreted."

Don't try this as a party trick, however. The drooling is often followed by hours of nausea, dizziness, and other unpleasant symptoms. Other plants that make you drool include the betel nut, which produces bright red saliva, as well as the Calabar bean and pencil tree, both of which also bring on unpleasant and sometimes fatal side effects.

SANGRE DE DRAGO
Croton lechleri

A shrub in the Euphoribiaceae family that oozes a thick red sap. The "blood" is used by some Amazon tribes to stop bleeding and treat other medical ailments.

PTEROCARPUS TREE
Pterocarpus erinaceus

Secretes a dark red resin that is used as a dye. The wood can be used to produce fine wood products; its leaves make good feed for cattle; and it may have some medicinal qualities.

DRACO
Daemonorops draco

Grows in southeast Asia; the reddish brown resin it excretes has been collected and sold in small, solid chunks as "red rock opium." Poison control centers and law enforcement agencies in the United States started seeing the substance on the streets in the late 1990s. However, laboratory tests confirmed that it has no hallucinogenic properties and certainly contains no opium.

During slobber weed's salivary action one or two pints of saliva, and even more, may be secreted.

Whistling Thorn Acacia

ACACIA DREPANOLOBIUM

One of the most wicked of the hundreds of acacias found throughout the world, this scrubby East African tree employs painful, three-inch thorns to keep browsers away from its lacy leaves. It is also host to a band of aggressive, stinging ants.

Four different species of ants have taken up residence in these trees, although they can't occupy the same tree without going to war with each other. They live in the swollen bases of acacia thorns, which they enter by chewing a hole through the thorn. That small hole creates the strange whistling sound that the tree makes in the wind.

FAMILY:
Fabaceae or Leguminosae

HABITAT:
Dry tropics, Kenya

NATIVE TO:
Africa

COMMON NAME:
Whistling thorn

The ants are not only ferocious; they're organized, too. Small militias patrol the branches looking for predators. They will swarm over a giraffe or other grazing animal to keep it from destroying their home. Other ants selectively prune the tree, allowing new growth only near their colonies so that they can enjoy the

The little zombies carry the acacia seeds around as if they were their own dead, helping to disperse the seeds and start the next generation.

tree's nectar. The ants will also chew climbing vines and other invasive plants down to stumps. If a tree occupied by a rival colony stretches its branches too close, the ants will decimate half of their own tree to keep the canopies from touching and creating a bridge to enemy territory.

And when the tribes do fight, they fight to the death. Researchers once tied the branches of neighboring trees together to provoke a conflict, and the ant corpses were piled a half-inch deep on the ground the next morning.

Meet the Relatives Some species, including *Acacia verticillata,* secrete a chemical that induces necrophoresis, or corpse-carrying behavior, in ants. The little zombies carry the acacia seeds around as if they were their own dead, helping to disperse the seeds and start the next generation. Many also have thorns; the cat claw acacia, *A. greggii,* is sometimes called the wait-a-minute bush because its prickles will grab hold of a hiker and refuse to let go.

GUESS WHO'S COMING TO DINNER

Plants don't just arm themselves with poisons and thorns. Some of them enlist the help of insects as well. Many seemingly innocuous plants act as host to stinging ants, wasps, and other creatures, providing them food and shelter in exchange for their services.

VALLEY OAK   *Quercus lobata*

Many oak trees host species of wasps, but California's valley oak is one of the best-known and most hospitable of all the oaks. The process begins when a wasp lays an egg on an oak leaf. The plant cells start multiplying at an unusually high rate, forming a kind of protective cocoon called a gall. Eventually the egg hatches into a larva, and the gall, which can get to be the size of a baseball, becomes a home to the larva and also gives it something to eat. The larvae emerge as full-grown wasps.

One species of wasp causes the valley oak to form small galls that drop off the tree. The galls can jump around for a few days as the wasp inside tries to break free, earning them the name "jumping oak galls."

FIGS
Ficus spp.

The relationship between figs and wasps is one of the most complicated in the plant kingdom. Figs don't actually produce fruit—that fleshy, juicy appendage that people eat is actually more like a swollen bit of stem with the remnants of the flower inside and a tiny opening at one end. Fig wasps, which can be as small as ants, breed inside this fruit-like structure. Once they have bred, the pregnant female flies to another fig, crawls inside, pollinating it in the process, and lays her eggs. She usually dies inside the fig after her work is done. The larva munch on the fig as they grow, and once they reach full size, they mate with each other. The male chews a hole through the fig to allow the female to escape, and then he dies, having served his only purpose in life. After the wasps are gone, the "fruit" continues to ripen, eventually becoming a food source for birds and humans alike.

Fig lovers may wonder if they've been eating wasp corpses all this time; in fact, many commercial fig varieties don't require pollination at all and others are only pollinated by wasps but don't host the eggs.

MEXICAN JUMPING BEANS
Sebastiana pavoniana

Jumping beans are actually the seeds of a shrub native to Mexico. A small, brown moth lays its egg on the seedpod, and the egg grows into a larva that chews its way into the seedpod then closes the hole with the silk it produces as it grows. The larva is sensitive to warmth and will start to twitch if the seed is held in the hand. After several months, the larva will form a pupa and then emerge as an adult, which will live for only a few days.

ANT PLANT *Hydnophytum formicarum*

This southeast Asian plant is an epiphyte, meaning that it grows on another tree for support. The base of the plant swells and forms a large hollow space that provides a home to an entire colony of ants. The ants build multichambered apartments, with a separate space for the queen, a nursery for their young, and a space where they can deposit their garbage. In exchange for providing a home for the ants, the plant sustains itself with the nutrients from the ant's waste products.

RATTAN *Daemonorops* spp.

Rattans are palms that grow in tropical rain forests, where their long, sturdy stems are in great demand for cane and wicker furniture. A single plant can reach over five hundred feet tall, often relying on other trees for support. Ants make themselves at home in the bases of rattan plants, and if they sense that the plant is under attack, they will beat their heads against the plant, causing the whole structure to rattle and shake. Once they've raised the alarm, ant colonies have been known to go on the attack, vigorously defending their home against rattan harvesters.

White Snakeroot

EUPATORIUM RUGOSUM
(SYN. AGERATINA ALTISSIMA)

Frontier life was harsh enough without the frightening possibility that fresh milk, butter, or meat could be contaminated by a deadly plant. Milk sickness was an all-too-common hazard of early farm life in America: entire families succumbed to the disease after suffering from symptoms that included weakness, vomiting, tremors, and delirium. Cattle also showed symptoms of the disease. Horses and cows would stagger around until they died, and farmers stood by helplessly, not realizing that a plant the cattle grazed on was to blame. The disease was so common that the names Milk Sick Ridge, Milk Sick Cove, and Milk Sick Holler are still attached to places in the South where the disease was rampant.

One of the most famous victims of milk sickness was Nancy Hanks Lincoln, mother of Abraham Lincoln. She fought the disease for a week but finally succumbed, as did her aunt and uncle and several other people in the small town of Little Pigeon Creek, Indiana. She died in 1818 at the age of thirty-four, leaving behind nine-year-old

FAMILY:
Asteraceae (or Compositae)

HABITAT:
Woodlands, thickets, meadows, and pastures

NATIVE TO:
North America

COMMON NAME:
White sanicle

Abraham Lincoln and his sister, Sarah. Lincoln's father built the coffins himself; young Abraham helped by carving the pegs for his mother's casket.

During the nineteenth century a few doctors and farmers independently discovered that white snakeroot was the cause of this illness, but news traveled slowly in those days. An Illinois doctor named Anna Bixby noticed the seasonality of the disease and speculated that it might have to do with the emergence of a particular plant in summer. She wandered the fields until she found white snakeroot, and she fed the weed to a calf to confirm that it caused the disease. She led a campaign to eradicate the plant from her community and almost eliminated milk sickness in that area by about 1834. Unfortunately, her attempts to notify authorities fell on deaf ears, perhaps because women doctors were not taken seriously.

One of the most famous victims of milk sickness, caused by white snakeroot, was Nancy Hanks Lincoln, mother of Abraham Lincoln.

Another early discovery was made by a farmer named William Jerry in Madison County, Illinois, in 1867, who realized that the disease occurred after his cattle grazed on white snakeroot, but it was not until the 1920s that white snakeroot was widely recognized as the cause. Eventually farmers learned to fence their cattle or eradicate the weed from pastures to prevent the disease.

White snakeroot grows to four feet tall and produces small, white clusters of flowers similar in shape to Queen Anne's lace. The plant is still found in the woods across eastern North America and throughout the South. The toxic ingredient, tremetol, remains active even after the plant has dried, making it a threat in hayfields as well as pastures.

Meet the Relatives Joe-pye weed, *Eupatorium purpureum,* a popular plant in butterfly gardens, and boneset, *E. perfoliatum,* which was once used as a laxative and as a treatment for fever and flu are both related to white snakeroot.

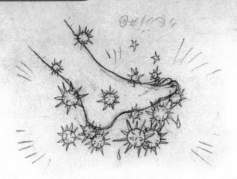

DON'T TREAD ON ME

Some plants get around by hitching a ride on an animal or an unsuspecting hiker. These plants are the most aggressive in the plant kingdom, practically leaping out to sink their teeth into a bare ankle or grab the tail of a golden retriever. The tiny, fishhook-like barbs mean that the more you pull on them, the more embedded they will become.

JUMPING CHOLLA	*Cylindropuntia fulgida* or
TEDDY BEAR CHOLLA	*C. bigelovii*

Cacti native to the southwestern United States. Hikers swear that the plants reach out and grab boots and pants legs. But in fact the spines are so strong that even the slightest grip is enough to cause one segment of the plant to break away. Don't try pulling it out; it will only stick to your hand. Experienced travelers carry a comb and use it to brush the plant away in one swift, painful motion.

GRAPPLE PLANT OR DEVIL'S CLAW   *Harpagophytum procumbens*

A tough, perennial vine found in South Africa. Its barbed seedpod can reach several inches in diameter, and each spine resembles a grappling hook, earning it its name. The plant produces beautiful pink flowers that resemble morning glory, but its oversized and painful seeds make it a menace for farmers and ranchers grazing livestock. Grapple plant does try to make up for the pain it causes: extracts of the roots have become a popular alternative remedy for treating pain and inflammation.

UNICORN PLANT   *Proboscidea louisianica, P. altheaefolia,* or *P. parviflora*

Native to the southern and western United States, this plant sprawls along the ground and resembles a squash vine. It sports showy pink or yellow trumpet-shaped blossoms that produce a seedpod with long, curved hooks that easily attach to shoes or hooves. The seed itself is covered in smaller, sharp spines. Also called devil's claw, devil's horn, or ram's horn

MOUSE TRAP TREE   *Uncarina grandidieri*

A small tree native to Madagascar, popular among tropical plant enthusiasts and found in botanical gardens throughout the United States. It produces gorgeous three-inch-long yellow flowers that give way to green fruit covered in otherwordly spines. Each spine has a tiny hook on the end; as the fruit dries, the remaining seedpod becomes a real hazard.

It could certainly snare a mouse, and humans who have been caught in its grip report that attempting to remove the seedpods is like getting caught in a Chinese finger trap.

FOXTAIL *Hordeum murinum*

A species of wild barley that produces the long, barbed seed heads that get embedded in dogs' fur in summer. However, the common name "foxtail" is also applied to a number of grasses that have similar seed heads. For example, ripgut grass (*Bromus diandrus*) is so tough that it can perforate the stomach lining of animals and actually kill them.

Foxtails sport tiny barbs that once embedded under the skin can be impossible to see and difficult to remove. The outer coating of the seedpods contains a bacterium that makes it easier for the barbs to work into the skin and even travel through the body. Dogs are the most susceptible; veterinarians have found foxtails inside their brains, lungs, and spinal cords.

COCKLEBUR *Xanthium strumarium*

A widespread summer weed in the aster family; it is native to North America but has become invasive worldwide. Cocklebur produces small seedpods covered in thorns, and although the pods are not difficult to remove, they have been known to ruin the wool of grazing sheep. The seeds are poisonous, and while most humans would not be tempted to munch on them, they can kill livestock.

BURDOCK *Arctium lappa, A. minus,* others

Produces thistle-shaped burrs that grab clothing and fur; leaves and stems irritate the skin. Burdock burrs are comparatively easy to remove, but they have the same fishhook structure of other stickers and grapples. This structure caught the attention of George de Mestral, the Swiss engineer who based his invention, Velcro, on the burdock burrs he found in his dog's fur after a walk.

SAND BURR AND GRASS BURR *Cenchrus echinatus* and *C. incertus*

These invasive grasslike plants have naturalized across the southern United States. They conceal themselves in lawns and produce small, sharp stickers that torture picnickers and punish children who dare to run across the yard barefoot. The burrs flourish in sandy soil with low fertility. They can irritate the eyes and lips of livestock, causing ulcers that can get infected. Control is difficult; some Southerners exact revenge by brewing sand burr wine with the burrs, grape juice, sugar, and Champagne yeast.

*The outer coating of the seedpods
contains a bacterium that makes it easier
for the barbs to work into the skin and
even travel through the body.
Dogs are the most susceptible; veterinarians
have found foxtails inside their brains,
lungs, and spinal cords.*

Yew

TAXUS BACCATA

I n 1240 Bartholomaeus Anglicus described the yew in his encyclopedia, *On the Properties of Things,* as "a tree with venim and poison." It's fitting, perhaps, that this highly toxic tree has come to be known as the graveyard tree in England. The plant earned that name not for its ability to send people to an early grave, but because Roman invaders began offering church services in the shade of yew trees, hoping that this would appeal to the pagan population. Today ancient yew trees are still found near churches in the English countryside.

FAMILY:
Taxaceae

HABITAT:
Temperate forests

NATIVE TO:
Europe, northwest Africa, Middle East, parts of Asia

COMMON NAMES:
Common yew, European or English yew

The sight of these yew trees in cemeteries inspired Alfred, Lord Tennyson, to write, "Thy fibres net the dreamless head / Thy roots are wrapt about the bones." In fact, an ancient churchside yew growing in the English village of Selborne was toppled during a storm in 1990, and the bones of the long-ago dead were found tangled in its roots.

The yew is a slow-growing evergreen that can live two or three centuries, but it is difficult to date mature trees because the dense wood doesn't always produce rings. The fine, needlelike leaves and red fruit make it an attractive landscape tree that can easily reach seventy feet in height. In England yews are often pruned to form a formal hedge; the Hampton Court Palace's legendary three-hundred-year-old hedge maze is now planted almost entirely with yew.

An ancient churchside yew growing in the English village of Selborne was toppled during a storm in 1990, and the bones of the long-ago dead were found tangled in its roots.

Every part of the yew is poisonous with the exception of the flesh of its red berrylike fruit (called an aril), and even that contains a toxic seed. The aril itself is slightly sweet, making it a temptation for children. Eating just a few seeds or a handful of leaves will bring on gastrointestinal symptoms, a dangerous drop in pulse rate, and possible heart failure. One medical manual mournfully noted that "many victims never described their symptoms" because they were found dead. Yews pose a particular hazard to pets and livestock. A veterinary medicine article stated that "often, the first evidence of yew toxicosis is unexpected death."

In Caesar's *Gallic Wars*, suicide by yew became a way to avoid facing defeat. Catuvolcus, king of a tribe who lived in what is now Belgium, was "worn out by age . . . unable to endure the fatigue either of war or flight" and "destroyed himself with the juice of the yew-tree." Pliny the Elder wrote that "travelers' vessels" made of yew wood and filled with wine could poison people who drank from them.

But before ripping that yew tree out of the garden, consider this: In the early 1960s a team of researchers from the National Cancer Institute discovered that yew extract had potent antitumor properties. Now the drug paclitaxel, or Taxol, is used to fight ovarian, breast, and lung cancers and shows promise for many others. Companies like Limehurst Ltd. collect hedge clippings from English gardens for the pharmaceutical industry. Research indicates that yew trees even secrete the drug into the dirt, opening up the possibility that cancer-fighting compounds can be extracted without harming the trees.

Meet the Relatives   Relatives include Japanese yew, *Taxus cuspidata,* which is native to Japan but grows throughout North America, Pacific or western yew, *T. brevifolia,* found in the western United States, and Canadian yew, *T. canadensis,* found in Canada and the eastern United States, which is also called American yew or ground hemlock.

End Notes

Antidote

Throughout the twentieth century, syrup of ipecac was recommended as a treatment for accidental poisoning. Ipecac is made from the roots of *Psychotria ipecacuanha,* a flowering shrub in Brazil. The syrup proved to be a powerful emetic, causing violent vomiting that might bring up the poison. Ipecac syrup eventually made its way into the medicine chest of every family with young children as a remedy for accidental poisoning.

However, the American Academy of Pediatrics and other medical groups now discourage the use of ipecac except if recommended by a doctor or poison control center. The syrup is abused by people with bulimia; in fact, it contributed to the death of singer Karen Carpenter. Ipecac has also been used in a few high-profile poisoning cases in which parents poison their children to get attention, a syndrome called Munchausen syndrome by proxy. Doctors also have more effective treatments for poisoning cases and believe that home use of ipecac may delay better treatment and mask symptoms. Instead, they recommend calling a poison control center or seeking immediate medical attention.

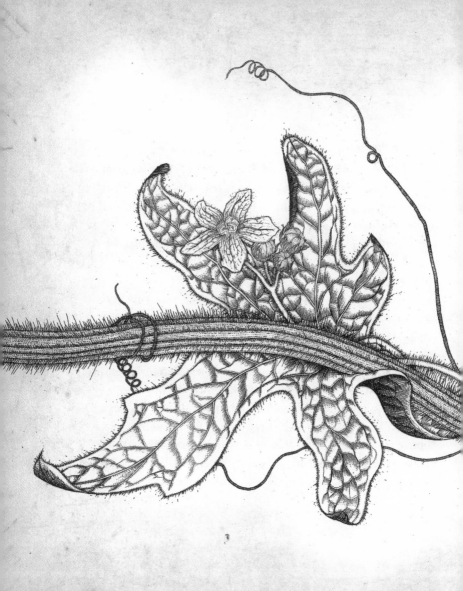

Briony

Briony Morrow-Cribbs creates copper etchings, fine bound books, and ceramic "cabinets of curiosity" that reflect her fascination with the ways in which the rational language of science meets the grotesque and absurd natural world. A graduate of the Emily Carr Institute of Art and Design, Morrow-Cribbs's work has been exhibited around the world. She resides in Brattleboro, Vermont, and is represented by the Davidson Gallery in Seattle. She is also the cofounder of Twin Vixen Press.

Briony shares her name with a wicked plant, *B. cretica.* Native to central and eastern Europe, this sturdy, twining vine produces red berries that cause vomiting, dizziness, and even respiratory failure. White bryony, *B. alba,* has been called "the kudzu of the Pacific Northwest" for its invasive behavior in that region. All plants in the *Bryonia* genus are poisonous to humans and live-stock; common names include snakeweed, bastard turnip, and devil turnip.

Jonathon

THE ARTIST

Brooklyn-based artist Jonathon Rosen's clients include Tim Burton, *I.D.* magazine, *Popular Science, Details, Sony, Outside* magazine, *Psychology Today, New York Times Magazine, Screwgun Records, Salon, Rolling Stone, Fortune,* MTV, *Time* magazine, and *Mother Jones,* among others. He has authored and illustrated two books, *Intestinal Fortitude* and *Birth of Machine Consciousness,* and his work has been collected by the New York Metropolitan Museum, David Cronenberg, and Si Newhouse.

Poison Gardens

ALNWICK POISON GARDENS

This garden in Northumberland, England, is surely the best place in the world to see wicked plants. Fans of the Harry Potter movies will recognize the medieval Alnwick Castle, which served as Hogwarts in the first two films. In the gardens surrounding the castle is an elaborate poison garden where henbane and belladonna flourish alongside tobacco and a caged cannabis specimen. Well worth a visit. Check www.alnwick garden.com to find out more, or call (01665) 511350.

BOTANICAL GARDEN OF PADUA

The world's oldest university botanical garden is situated near Venice in Padova, Italy. It includes an impressive collection of poisonous plants. Find out more at www.ortobotanico.unipd.it/eng/index.htm, or call +39 049 8272119.

CHELSEA PHYSIC GARDEN

This walled, centuries-old apothecaries' garden in the heart of London, includes a number of medicinal and poison plants, as well as a fascinating "order bed" garden that shows how families of plants are related to each other. Go to www.chelseaphysicgarden.co.uk, or call (020) 7352 5646.

MONTREAL BOTANICAL GARDEN

This world-class botanical garden includes a small, fenced toxic plant garden and a medicinal garden. They even include poison ivy in their collection. Check out www2.ville.montreal.qc.ca/jardin/en/menu.htm, or call 001 514 872 1400.

MUTTER MUSEUM

The College of Physicians of Philadelphia has a museum devoted to our sometimes gruesome medical history. In addition to antique medical equipment and pathological specimens, there is a medicinal garden filled with powerful plants. Visit www.collphyphil.org or call 001 215 563 3737.

W. C. MUENSCHER POISONOUS PLANTS GARDEN

Cornell University maintains a poisonous plant garden in Ithaca, New York, as part of its veterinary school. Most of the plants will be familiar to North American gardeners; the goal is to help familiarize students of veterinary medicine with the plants that animals are most likely to encounter. Visit www.plantations.cornell.edu, or call 001 607 255 2400.

---

*Visit www.wickedplants.com for links
to poisonous plant databases, photos of
poisonous plants, and more.*

Bibliography

POISONOUS PLANT RESOURCES AND IDENTIFICATION GUIDES

Brickell, Christopher. *The American Horticultural Society A–Z Encyclopedia of Garden Plants.* New York: DK Publishing, 2004.

Brown, Tom, Jr. *Tom Brown's Guide to Wild Edible and Medicinal Plants.* New York: Berkley Books, 1985.

Bruneton, Jean. *Toxic Plants Dangerous to Humans and Animals.* Secaucus, NJ: Lavoisier Publishing, 1999.

Foster, Steven. *Venomous Animals and Poisonous Plants.* New York: Houghton Mifflin, 1994.

Frohne, Dietrich. *Poisonous Plants: A Handbook for Doctors, Pharmacists, Toxicologists, Biologists and Veterinarians.* Portland, OR: Timber Press, 2005.

Kingsbury, John. *Poinsonous Plants of the United States and Canada.* Englewood Cliffs, NJ: Prentice Hall, 1964.

Klaassen, Curtis. *Casarett & Doull's Toxicology: The Basic Science of Poisons.* New York: McGraw-Hill Professional, 2001.

Turner, Nancy. *Common Poisonous Plants and Mushrooms of North America.* Portland, OR: Timber Press, 1991.

Van Wyk, Ben-Erik. *Medicinal Plants of the World.* Portland, OR: Timber Press, 2004.

FURTHER READING

Adams, Jad. *Hideous Absinthe: A History of the Devil in a Bottle.* Madison: University of Wisconsin Press, 2004.

Anderson, Thomas. *The Poison Ivy, Oak & Sumac Book: A Short Natural History and Cautionary Account.* Ukiah, CA: Acton Circle Publishing, 1995.

Attenborough, David. *The Private Life of Plants: A Natural History of Plant Behaviour.* Princeton, NJ: Princeton University Press, 1995.

Balick, Michael. *Plants, People and Culture: The Science of Ethnobotany.* New York: Scientific American Library, 1996.

Booth, Martin. *Cannabis: A History.* New York: St. Martin's Press, 2003.

Booth, Martin. *Opium: A History.* New York: Thomas Dunne, 1998.

Brickhouse, Thomas. *The Trial and Execution of Socrates.* New York: Oxford University Press, 2001.

Cheeke, Peter R. *Toxicants of Plant Origin.* Vol. I, *Alkaloids.* Boca Raton, FL: CRC Press, 1989.

Conrad, Barnaby. *Absinthe: History in a Bottle.* San Francisco: Chronicle Books, 1988.

Crosby, Donald. *The Poisoned Weed : Plants Toxic to Skin.* New York: Oxford University Press, 2004.

D'Amato, Peter. *The Savage Garden: Cultivating Carnivorous Plants.* Berkeley, CA: Ten Speed Press, 1998.

Everist, Selwyn. *Poisonous Plants of Australia.* Sydney, Australia: Angus and Robertson, 1974.

Gately, Iain. *Tobacco: The Story of How Tobacco Seduced the World.* New York: Grove Press, 2001.

Gibbons, Bob. *The Secret Life of Flowers*. London: Blandford, 1990.

Grieve, M. *A Modern Herbal*. Vols. 1 and 2. New York: Dover, 1982.

Hardin, James. *Human Poisoning from Native and Cultivated Plants*. Durham, NC: Duke University Press, 1974.

Hartzell, Hal, Jr. *The Yew Tree: A Thousand Whispers*. Eugene, OR: Hulogosi, 1991.

Hodgson, Barbara. *In the Arms of Morpheus: The Tragic History of Laudanum, Morphine, and Patent Medicines*. Buffalo, NY: Firefly Books, 2001.

Hodgson, Barbara. *Opium: A Portrait of the Heavenly Demon*. San Francisco: Chronicle Books, 1999.

Jane, Duchess of Northumberland. *The Poison Diaries*. New York: Harry N. Abrams, 2006.

Jolivet, Pierre. *Interrelationship between Insects and Plants*. Boca Raton, FL: CRC Press, 1998.

Lewin, Louis. *Phantastica: A Classic Survey on the Use and Abuse of Mind-Altering Plants*. Rochester, VT: Park Street Press, 1998.

Macinnis, Peter. *Poisons: From Hemlock to Botox to the Killer Bean of Calabar*. New York: Arcade Publishing, 2005.

Mayor, Adrienne. *Greek Fire, Poison Arrows, and Scorpion Bombs: Biological and Chemical Warfare in the Ancient World*. Woodstock, NY: Overlook Duckworth, 2003.

Meinsesz, Alexandre. *Killer Algae*. Chicago: University of Chicago Press, 1999.

Ogren, Thomas. *Allergy-Free Gardening*. Berkeley, CA: Ten Speed Press, 2000.

Pavord, Anna. *The Naming of Names: The Seach for Order in the World of Plants*. New York: Bloomsbury, 2005.

Pendell, Dale. *Pharmakodynamis Stimulating Plants, Potions, and Herbcraft: Excitantia and Empathogenica*. San Francisco: Mercury House, 2002.

Rocco, Fiammetta. *Quinine: Malaria and the Quest for a Cure That Changed the World*. New York: HarperCollins, 2003.

Schiebinger, Londa. *Plants and Empire: Colonial Bioprospecting in the Atlantic World*. Cambridge, MA: Harvard University Press, 2004.

Spinella, Marcello. *The Psychopharmacology of Herbal Medicine: Plant Drugs That Alter Mind, Brain, and Behavior*. Cambridge, MA: The MIT Press, 2001.

Stuart, David. *Dangerous Garden: The Quest for Plants to Change Our Lives*. Cambridge, MA: Harvard University Press, 2004.

Sumner, Judith. *The Natural History of Medicinal Plants*. Portland, OR: Timber Press, 2000.

Talalaj, S., D. Talalaj, and J. Talalaj. *The Strangest Plants in the World*. London: Hale, 1992.

Timbrell, John. *The Poison Paradox*. New York: Oxford University Press, 2005.

Todd, Kim. *Chrysalis: Maria Sibylla Merian and the Secrets of Metamorphosis*. New York: Harcourt, 2007.

Tompkins, Peter. *The Secret Life of Plants*. New York: Harper Perennial, 1973.

Wee, Yeow Chin. *Plants That Heal, Thrill and Kill*. Singapore: SNP Reference, 2005.

Wilkins, Malcom. *Plantwatching: How Plants Remember, Tell Time, Form Relationships, and More*. New York: Facts on File, 1988.

Wittles, Betina. *Absinthe: Sip of Seduction; A Contemporary Guide*. Denver, CO: Speck Press, 2003.